Percy Thrower's Gardening Year

Line drawings by Norman Barber

HAMLYN

London · New York · Sydney · Toronto

First published in 1973 by
The Hamlyn Publishing Group Limited
London · New York · Sydney · Toronto
Astronaut House, Feltham, Middlesex, England
Second impression, 1976

This book is an abridged version of
In Your Garden with Percy Thrower, also
published by The Hamlyn Publishing Group Limited

Printed in Great Britain by Cox & Wyman Limited,
London, Reading and Fakenham.
Set in 10 on 11pt Intertype Times

Cover illustration by courtesy of *Amateur Gardening*

Contents

Present-day Gardening

Gardening is an ever-growing interest. Few houses, nowadays, are built without their accompanying garden, and many thousands of young people each year find that they have a garden for the first time in their lives.

Generally speaking, everyone is looking for easier and better ways of running their gardens. The tendency is to concentrate on permanent plants that will provide colour throughout the year in one form or another with little maintenance involved and to rely less on bedding plants like geraniums, salvias and lobelias.

More and more, too, garden owners are using ground-cover plants to keep down weeds and reduce work – plants like the heathers (ericas), periwinkle (vinca), hostas, bergenias, *Stachys macrantha* and the herbaceous geraniums. If ground-cover plants are introduced into the garden in a sensible way and balanced with plants grown primarily for their colour and other decorative features, then you will find that the garden loses nothing in interest and beauty.

One of the most interesting developments in recent years has been the widespread adoption of 'island-bed' planting for all kinds of plants from shrubs to herbaceous plants and annuals, these often being very attractively mixed together. There are several advantages in this kind of display: you can shape them to suit your garden's overall layout; you can view the plants all round, and it makes routine cultivations and plant care quite a lot easier.

An awful headache for many people moving into a completely new home is to know how to start to make a garden from the rough site the builder will have left behind him. My advice would be to sort out, first of all, any bricks, stones and rubbish which may be lying around and place these on one side for later path making. Next, dig over the whole plot or, better still, either hire a cultivator or get a garden contractor to work the ground over initially and level it. This will save time and energy and leave you free to get on with other jobs. If the soil is heavy it is advisable to work in peat, garden compost or straw at this stage to improve its texture and to aid free drainage. Light soils, too, benefit from such dressings for the texture of these can also be improved in this way and their moisture-holding capacity is increased.

My next recommendation would be to put the whole area down to grass seed. A suitable time is between late March and April in the South and in April or May in the Midlands or North. Better still, though, is August or September for at this time there are unlikely to be periods of prolonged drought just when the young grass is becoming established. Within a few weeks from sowing there will be a pleasant green sward around the house and you will then have time to think what else you would like to do.

Flower beds and borders, planting holes for trees, paths, a site for a pool perhaps – all these can be cut out of the grass at a later stage when your plans have been finalised. The attraction of making a garden this way is that you do not have to look at rather depressing bare soil for a long period and it gives you all the time in the world to develop your garden at your own pace without it looking unattractive in the process.

A common fault in garden making is to try and cram

An attractive combination of foliage plants and paving

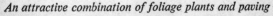

too much into a small area. This is never successful and I would strongly recommend concentrating on a few really good features which will be in keeping with their surroundings. And when you buy plants, make sure that they are of high quality. There is no falser economy than to buy inferior plants for not only is it money which is wasted in the long run but time as well, for the lack of success which may follow such purchases can take a year or so to show.

One of the first jobs in a new garden is the laying of paths for these are an absolute necessity – to reach, say, the vegetable garden, the greenhouse, or just to take you to a special garden feature like a small rock garden or pool. Any soil dug out during the construction of the path can be used in other parts of the garden, and the broken bricks, stones, ashes or other rough material which are used to form the base of the path put in its place. The top layer could be gravel, tarmac, concrete, paving stones or crazy paving. If paving stones are laid, set these on a sand base and secure each one with four or five blobs of cement on the base. Such a path always looks attractive.

I like to see small planting areas left in paving where thymes, armerias, dianthus, sempervivums and similar plants can be grown. This helps to give the garden cohesion.

Another attractive feature is a sink garden, especially if one positions it near the house where it can be viewed as one walks up to the front door or where it can be enjoyed from inside the house. Many popular rock-garden plants of small size and with slow growth are suitable for such a feature – things like *Phlox douglasii* and its varieties, *Primula marginata*, some of the saxifrages and an enormous range of sempervivums, the pretty *Penstemon rupicola*, dwarf narcissi, crocuses, dwarf irises, and a host of other plants, with dwarf conifers like the popular *Juniperus communis compressa* to give added interest.

Something which is often overlooked is that the soil in

the typical small garden – usually packed with trees, shrubs and other plants – becomes impoverished after a time. It must be kept in good heart by applying humus-forming material like peat, garden compost or farmyard manure, and providing balanced plant foods in the form of fertilisers. The best time to feed plants is in the spring when they are beginning to come into growth.

The traditional planting seasons for many plants have been vastly altered, if not stood on their heads, by the large-scale introduction of container-grown plants, for these can be planted at any time of year, when weather and soil conditions are suitable. Trees, shrubs, conifers, roses, border plants and fruit trees can all be bought in containers nowadays. Quite apart from the advantage of being able to plant at virtually any time, it has also given less experienced gardeners the opportunity to see so many flowering plants in bloom – before they make their final choice. Previously, it was a question of ordering from a catalogue and waiting for results. The sale of plants through garden centres and similar outlets has really given gardening a new face, for in addition to seeing a wide range of plants it is also possible to seek advice on what is right for your soil, what height particular plants will grow to eventually and things of that sort.

Three styles of paving suitable for garden use

There are a few simple rules which should be observed when you get container-grown plants home. First, give them a thorough watering before they are removed from their containers. Secondly, remove them from their containers carefully, so that the roots are not disturbed. Thirdly, do not plant them too deeply. Mix peat with the soil and add a little bonemeal or general fertiliser but take care that the fertiliser used does not come in direct contact with the roots. Make the soil firm around the plant and water in well. If a dry period follows, the plant should be watered again about a week later.

In all but the smallest of gardens I feel an area should be screened off for growing vegetables. Fruit too, although this does depend on the kind of fruit you wish to grow and how it is grown (or trained) in relation to the space you have available. You could grow apples or pears as cordons or espaliers to form a barrier between the vegetable and flower garden – an admirable way to kill two birds with one stone for the blossom is attractive and the trained forms produce high-quality fruits when well looked after.

The vegetable garden should be used to produce the favourite vegetables of the family, not just stock produce like potatoes, cabbages and cauliflowers but those which are more difficult to buy or have got to be used fresh – young carrots, French beans, broad beans, runner beans, young beetroots, lettuces, radishes and peas. There are also Brussels sprouts, savoy cabbages, broccoli, leeks and celery to consider. The range depends entirely on the size of your garden and your requirements. One thing is certain, bought vegetables – or fruit for that matter – bear no comparison with home-raised produce for flavour.

Always pay attention to continuity and succession with vegetables for there is no profit in having a glut at one moment and little or nothing at another. Intercropping – growing quick-maturing crops between those which need longer to mature – is also profitable. With a little forethought it should be possible to have something from the vegetable garden throughout most of the year.

You can advance the season of many crops by making use of plastic cloches, getting produce two or three weeks earlier in the case of lettuces, peas, onions and carrots.

I suppose the most popular top fruits must be apples and pears, and with space a problem in many gardens nowadays, there is every inducement to grow them as cordons, espaliers, dwarf pyramids (for apples) and dwarf bushes. Appropriate dwarfing rootstocks are available and it is quite easy to obtain the right kind of stock for your conditions.

I believe in always using the walls of the house and garage whenever possible to grow fruit. A north-facing wall is ideal for a fan-trained Morello cherry, and a sunny wall is excellent for peaches, nectarines and plums.

Soft fruits are an excellent proposition even in a quite small garden for they take up relatively little space and give an excellent return. The most popular kind is undoubtedly the strawberry, followed, I suppose, by the raspberry. Then there are the currants; black, red and

Cordon-trained apples are especially useful in a small garden

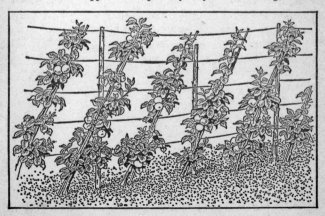

white, and gooseberries and loganberries, too, if you want something a little different.

I have quite a lot to say in this book about pest and disease control because this is such an important part of running a really successful garden or greenhouse. I would not wish to over-emphasise this aspect of the gardener's craft but it is, perhaps, timely to say that prevention is better than cure and that good hygiene in garden and greenhouse alike – and particularly in the latter with its enclosed environment – can mean that one avoids a whole host of troubles which afflict less prudent or careful gardeners. The other thing is to grow your plants really well for it is usually the weak or sickly plant which succumbs most easily to pest and disease attack.

Also, when using chemicals in a garden read the manufacturer's instructions carefully, and apply them at the right time. I will agree that it is not always easy for the inexperienced to remember just when to do this and that to prevent damage or an infestation, but it is worth going to some trouble to become well informed on the habits of the most troublesome pests and diseases and know the kind of symptoms to look for.

On timings it is a great help to keep a diary of when particular jobs are done so that this can be referred to in subsequent years. (Such a diary can be fascinating, too, if you also include such details as the flowering times of plants and the kind of results obtained, when seeds were sown or plantings made and other things of that nature.)

The other very important thing is to keep all garden chemicals well out of the way of children – preferably in a locked cupboard, but if this is not possible, at least on a high shelf in the garden shed.

Nowadays it is possible to buy multi-purpose sprays and dusts and these have made things much easier for all of us. Also, modern spraying equipment is easy to operate and light to handle for it is usual for plastic to be used as much as possible.

To have a greenhouse is to open up whole new avenues of enjoyment. To be able to grow plants independent of the weather and plan for interest during all the seasons is a wonderful extension of one's hobby – gardening. With modern equipment and greenhouses the gardener has many options open to him, these ranging from the warm greenhouse which, if fitted with labour-saving equipment, gives the gardener the most opportunities to be adventurous, to the cool greenhouse, the unheated greenhouse, the sun lounge or conservatory. Whichever you choose you can be certain that you will have a lot of pleasure. The only thing I would say on the question of choice is that a moderately heated greenhouse gives infinitely more scope to the gardener than an unheated one, but such decisions must be taken in the light of how much you are able or prepared to spend.

An important consideration when siting your greenhouse is convenience and access. In other words you should place it as near to the house as possible, bearing in mind that you want the best possible light conditions inside the greenhouse and the minimum of distance to walk from the house on cold winter nights and in wet weather. The other important consideration in this respect is the availability of electricity and gas services; electricity for obvious reasons because so much equipment, including lighting and heating, is controlled by this nowadays and gas because there is now a first-class natural gas greenhouse heater of completely new design in addition to the conventional gas-fired boiler heating piped water.

One last word; throughout the text I have referred to the use of loam in preparing composts. As everybody knows this is becoming more and more difficult to obtain so on occasions it may be necessary to substitute good topsoil – as infrequently as possible, though, I would hope.

January: week 1

FLOWERS

When the lawn is reasonably dry, sweep with a besom to scatter worm casts and remove dead grass. If the lawn was not given a topdressing in autumn do this now. Use a mixture of equal parts peat and loam at the rate of 4 lb. to the square yard, and push it backwards and forwards with the back of a rake to work it down into the turf.

Look carefully at trees, shrubs and roses planted last autumn and re-firm them if they have become loosened by wind or frost. Choose a day when the surface of the soil is fairly dry or it will become too compacted.

Now that the new season's catalogues are available it is interesting to go through them and note the new plants which are being offered.

FRUIT

Trees and bushes planted earlier may need firming in. Continue with planting when conditions are satisfactory.

If fruit trees have not already had their winter spray, do this as soon as possible.

Check all the grease bands put on older trees last autumn and renew the grease where necessary. It is also a

Spraying a young apple tree with tar oil wash to kill the overwintering eggs of insects and remove green algae

Opposite: *Potting up autumn-sown sweet peas separately in 3-in. pots using the John Innes No. 1 Potting Compost. Afterwards twiggy sticks are inserted around the edge of the pots to give the young plants the support they need*

good idea to make regular inspections of fruit in store and remove any that are rotten.

If outdoor vines were not pruned in December do this now. The method of pruning is similar to that of indoor vines (see p. 152), but less severe.

Sacking soaked in animal oil placed loosely around the base of trees will prevent mouse damage. Take care not to get the oil actually on the trunk as this could prove fatal. Another way of preventing mouse damage is to rub ordinary carbolic soap on the trunk of the tree.

VEGETABLES

Clear away the stems and roots of green vegetables which have finished and get on with winter cultivations. Heavy clay soil benefits from the action of frost and rain which helps to break down the large clods and makes it easier to get a fine tilth for seed beds.

Decide where root crops are going to be grown this season so that the chosen area can be left free of manure. Divide the vegetable garden into thirds, and manure one third of the total area each year. If farmyard manure is not available, use compost or peat as substitutes.

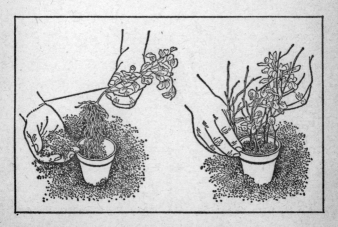

January: week 1

Put cloches over ground one intends to make into early seed beds. These will dry out the soil and bring sowing dates forward. Plastic cloches rather than glass ones are the most popular these days.

Inspect vegetables in store for signs of decay. Root vegetables can often be used if the decayed area is cut away at an early stage.

GREENHOUSE

This is an important time for chrysanthemum enthusiasts, for preparations should be made now to take cuttings. Place the chrysanthemum stools close to the glass to encourage the development of sturdy material for cuttings and prepare a cutting compost of 1 part loam, 2 parts granulated peat and 3 parts sharp sand.

Pay special attention to watering at this time of year to avoid a damp, cold atmosphere which could lead to trouble, particularly with calceolaria hybrids, cinerarias and cyclamen.

Bring more bulbs in pots from the plunge bed into the greenhouse for a succession of flowers. The cooler the house the better, for their introduction to warm conditions should be gradual to achieve even growth. Daffodils and hyacinths are liable to flop and will need staking.

Pot on the autumn-sown sweet peas, placing each seedling in a 3-in. pot of John Innes No. 1 Potting Compost.

If bulbs of *Lilium auratum* and *L. speciosum rubrum* were not potted up in October do this now.

Freesias will benefit from feeding with a little weak liquid manure. Indeed, most plants benefit from a feed at 10- to 14-day intervals.

Plants that have been in the home over Christmas and are showing signs of distress can be revived by a short spell in the greenhouse.

FLOWERS

If established lawns need renovating in any way, do this work now. Choose a day when the weather is open and the soil reasonably dry. Bumps and hollows in the lawn can be levelled out by lifting small areas of the turf and either adding or removing soil as appropriate. Where turf at the edge of a path or bed has become worn this can be made good by cutting away the damaged area and replacing it with new turves. It is best to cut a rectangle of the existing turf and move this to the edge, putting the patch behind it, as a narrow strip of new turf might not stay in position.

New lawns from turf can also be made at this time of year. Remember though that it is not always easy to purchase good quality turf, and very often it is infested with weeds, moss, leatherjackets or wireworms. Another disadvantage is the cost, for a lawn made from turf is about 75 per cent. more expensive than one from seed.

When seeds which you have ordered arrive, keep them in a cool, dry place until required, and protect them from mice. An old biscuit tin makes an excellent container and will keep the seeds in perfect condition.

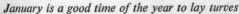

January is a good time of the year to lay turves

January: week 2

Prepare the ground for outdoor chrysanthemums by digging thoroughly and incorporating manure and a dusting of bonemeal and hoof and horn meal.

Slugs can damage carnations and pinks at this time, so put down slug bait if trouble is noticed.

FRUIT
Morello cherries trained as fans are excellent plants for a north-facing wall, being both decorative and profitable. They should be planted now.

Cuttings of currants and gooseberries may have become loosened by recent frosts. If so, firm them in again with the feet.

Paint outdoor vine rods with one of the proprietary sulphur dressings as a preventive against mildew, and sprinkle 4 oz. of general organic fertiliser around each plant.

VEGETABLES
Lift more strong roots of rhubarb for forcing, or cover them where they are growing with a bucket, covering this in turn with straw or leaves to keep out the frost.

When seed potatoes arrive put them in shallow trays to sprout, and keep in a frost-proof place.

Seeds of some early crops can be sown in heated

Inserting chrysanthemum cuttings around the edge of a 3-in. pot of cutting compost with the aid of a dibber. Four to six can be put in each pot

frames. These include carrots, onions and lettuces with radishes sown between them as these will be pulled before any of the other crops require more room.

GREENHOUSE

Wash the outside of the glass of your greenhouse and frames, especially if you live in an industrial area. This can make a tremendous difference to the amount of light the plants receive, which is rarely sufficient in the winter months, even with conditions at their best.

Do not be tempted by a few days of fine weather to sow seeds too early, for it is extremely important with seedlings that reasonable temperatures should be maintained. If it is not possible to maintain a temperature of at least 10°C. (50°F.) it is unwise to sow anything for the next few weeks.

Take cuttings of chrysanthemums, selecting shoots growing directly from the roots rather than the stem. Choose sturdy, short-jointed shoots about 3 in. long and trim them just below a leaf joint with a sharp knife. Remove the lower leaves and then dip the cuttings in rooting powder before inserting them in 3-in. pots of cutting compost (see p. 14). Place the pots in a propagating frame with a temperature of 7°C. (45°F.).

Late batches of cyclamen seedlings should be potted up into 3- or $3\frac{1}{2}$-in. pots.

Inspect hydrangeas for any sign of botrytis which can affect the terminal buds from which the flower stems will be produced. In such cases reduce the water supplies, keep the atmosphere dry and spray with thiram.

Remove flowers from plants of *Azalea indica* as soon as they begin to fade. When flowering has finished, repot the plants into a larger size if they are at present in 3-, 4-, or 5-in. pots and the same size if they are in 6- or 7-in. pots (having first teased away some of the old soil). Use a compost consisting of 2 parts peat and 1 part sand, and feed once every 14 days during spring and summer.

January: week 3

FLOWERS

If the weather is open during February and the soil in a workable condition, it is a good month to plant many herbaceous perennials, so the plants should be ordered now if they are to arrive in time. Of course, this does not apply to container-grown plants which can be planted at more or less any time of the year.

Useful plants for positions near the front of the border are *Sedum spectabile*, nepeta (catmint), *Physostegia* Vivid, the dwarf forms of solidago, *Tradescantia* Leonora, *Veronica incana* and varieties of *Dianthus allwoodii*.

If dahlia sites are prepared now, it will give any manure worked in a chance to become really well incorporated with the soil before planting in late spring. Dahlias are gross feeders and they like plenty of humus-forming material in the soil as well as bonemeal and hoof and horn meal.

Viburnum fragrans can be propagated this month or next by layering. Peg suitable low-growing branches down into the ground.

FRUIT

Tie in raspberry canes to the training wires, spacing them 9 in. apart. Where the canes are much higher than the top wire, cut them back to only a few inches above. It is unwise to allow them to grow more than 5 ft. high.

Examine apple trees for canker wounds, and if any are seen cut out the affected bark and wood until clean tissue is reached. Then paint over with white lead or bitumastic paint. This treatment can only be carried out on fairly thick branches, and any thin stems showing signs of canker should be cut right out.

Feed black currants with a general organic fertiliser at the rate of 4 to 6 oz. to each bush. Sprinkle it thinly on the soil and keep well away from the stems.

Now is a good time to prune gooseberries, unless you live in an area subject to bird damage, in which case wait

18

until next month. Generally, a moderate thinning is all that is necessary, but further details are given on p. 33.

VEGETABLES

In sheltered districts, especially in the South and West, some seed can now be sown under cloches. Early sowings should include lettuces, carrots, radishes, onions, round-seeded peas and broad beans.

Clean away any dead or decaying leaves from winter lettuce as these, if left, may give the botrytis fungus a chance to start its work of decay. Lettuces in frames should also be picked over.

If you have a frame, sow seed of cauliflower, a quick-maturing variety of cabbage and some lettuces, all for planting out later on. Care should be taken to sow the seed thinly for overcrowding encourages damping off.

If the site of the onion bed has now been chosen, a lot of good can be done by pricking over the surface when it is dry. This will help when the time comes to make a good tilth in March in preparation for seed sowing. Onions appreciate bonfire ash, and if this is available, spread it over the bed now and fork in lightly. Also, a dressing of bonemeal is beneficial.

Tying in raspberry canes to supporting wires. When properly trained, the canes should be spaced about 9 in. apart

January: week 3

GREENHOUSE

Strawberries in pots which have been in a cold frame until now should be brought into the greenhouse. Scrape away a little of the surface soil and topdress with John Innes No. 3 Potting Compost. The plants should then be stood on the staging or a shelf close to the glass where they will receive the maximum amount of light.

If onions have not already been sown in boxes for planting out later, do this as soon as possible. If seed was sown in December, the seedlings will probably be ready for pricking out into boxes of John Innes No. 1 Potting Compost. When onions are being grown for exhibition purposes it is better to prick out the seedlings singly at this stage into 3-in. pots for this way they can be transferred with the minimum of disturbance.

Do not sow tomato seeds early unless a minimum temperature of 16°C. (60°F.) can be maintained.

Look over chrysanthemum cuttings and remove any leaves which are decaying. More cuttings can be inserted as suitable material becomes available.

Prune established fuchsias now. All side growths on standards must be cut hard back to within two or three buds of the main stem, and bushes should be cut back fairly severely too.

Specimens of *Primula malacoides* can be moved into 5-in. pots if large plants are wanted.

Cuttings of perpetual-flowering carnations taken in December should have rooted now and can be potted into 3-in. pots of John Innes No. 1 Potting Compost. Keep conditions cool – 7°C. (45°F.) is quite adequate. Ventilate freely to prevent the air becoming damp and stuffy.

Topdress vine borders with well-rotted manure and give each plant 6 oz. of bonemeal.

FLOWERS

If some replanting is to be done in the herbaceous border, preparations should begin now. Those plants which are to be moved should be lifted and put on one side. If the clumps are placed close together and covered with straw they will keep in good condition for some time. The soil in the border can then be turned over to at least the depth of a spade, and manure, peat or compost worked in as digging proceeds. A good handful of bonemeal should be sprinkled along each yard of trench. This thorough preparation is well worth while because, once replanted, most herbaceous plants remain undisturbed for at least three years. I would make an exception in the case of Michaelmas daisies which I prefer to lift and divide annually. I find that I get stronger and larger spikes by doing this and the plants are less susceptible to mildew attack.

If sweet peas were sown out of doors in the autumn, place cloches over them as a precaution against the possibility of severe weather. Alternatively, twiggy sticks pushed in along the sides of the rows will provide some protection.

Prune ornamental trees where necessary, taking care not to cut out wood that will bear flowers in spring or early summer.

The flowers of hardy primulas and polyanthus are often damaged by birds and it is a good idea to protect these now while they are still in bud. Black cotton stretched across the plant is a good deterrent, or they can be sprayed with a bird repellent.

FRUIT

Newly planted black currants and raspberries should be pruned severely, the black currants to within 2 to 3 in. of the ground to encourage strong growths from below ground level. Young shoots removed when pruning can be inserted as hard-wood cuttings. Raspberries should be cut down to a prominent bud 6 to 9 in. above the ground.

January: week 4

In country districts bullfinches do a lot of damage to plums and damsons as the buds begin to swell. Unless something is done to check them the whole season's crop can be lost. Milk bottle tops make good bird scarers if threaded on black cotton. Alternatively, spray with a bird repellent.

Damsons, incidentally, make a very useful windbreak when planted on the east side of the garden. They should be grown as bush specimens or standards. The most suitable variety is Merryweather.

The buds on wall-trained peach trees in the South and in sheltered places in the West will soon begin to swell so spraying and cleaning should be completed as quickly as possible. Use a winter spray, preferably thiocyanate.

VEGETABLES
As soon as Brussels sprouts have been gathered, the stalks should be cleared from the ground, unless there is a shortage of purple-sprouting broccoli or kale. In this case, a few Brussels sprouts should be left to produce young shoots for gathering later on.

Do not be tempted to make outdoor sowings of veg-

Newly planted raspberries should be cut down to within about 9 in. of the ground. Make the cut just above a prominent bud

etables too early. There is probably a good deal of hard weather ahead.

Mice often damage early-sown peas and beans. Trapping or poisoning now can prevent a lot of damage later on, but if poison is used it must be kept away from children, animals and birds. As a precaution, place the poison in a drainpipe or cover it in some way.

GREENHOUSE

Seed sowing of a few half-hardy and tender plants can begin if a propagating frame is available but I prefer to wait a little. If you have a cold house you will not gain anything by early sowing.

Repot fuchsias which were pruned earlier. Shake away all the old soil and then put the plants in the smallest pots which will contain their roots.

Regal pelargoniums which are starting to grow may be potted on into pots which are one size larger if their existing pots are well filled with roots. With mature plants I remove most of the old soil and repot them in new compost using pots of the same size.

Take cuttings of perpetual-flowering carnations at any time between November and March. Use short, non-flowering sideshoots, preferably from mid-way up the stems. Make the cuttings 3 to 4 in. long and cut cleanly at the base. Root in sand in a propagating frame with a temperature of 16°C. (60°F.).

Remove dead leaves from pelargonium, fuchsia, heliotrope and coleus cuttings to prevent disease gaining a hold. Ventilate the greenhouse to keep the atmosphere buoyant.

Hydrangeas can be moved to a warmer position to encourage early flowers.

Water with particular care at this time of year, especially when plants are grown in plastic pots which hold water considerably longer than clay ones.

February: week 1

FLOWERS

Winter-flowering shrubs should be pruned as soon as they finish flowering. The Winter-flowering Jasmine, *Jasminum nudiflorum*, is one shrub in particular that benefits. Train in as many of the growths that have just finished flowering as are needed to cover the wall and cut the remainder back to three or four buds so that they make strong growths for flowering next winter. This is a splendid shrub for a north-facing wall, and the flowers can be cut for room decoration when cut blooms are scarce.

Trim back winter-flowering heathers as the blooms fade to prevent them becoming straggly. Use shears for this job.

This is a good time of year to make a small rock garden. An interesting home for alpine plants can be made with no more than six to eight stones of moderate size. These should be sited with care and the spaces between them filled with good soil – it is most important that it should be weed free – mixed with plenty of coarse grit and some peat. Never place such a rock garden under trees or in the shade but always in a sunny, open position. Good drainage is another necessity.

Preparing the ground for an early sowing of vegetables. 1. When sowing seeds a fine tilth is essential and this is achieved by careful raking to break up the surface soil and remove any debris. 2. When the soil is sufficiently fine, drills should be drawn out with a hoe using a line as a guide. 3. Seed should be sown thinly because overcrowding will lead to weak plants

Dahlia tubers in store should be examined periodically, and if there are signs of mould, dusted with flowers of sulphur. Make sure they are protected against frost.

FRUIT

Morello cherries growing against walls should be trained in such a way that the growths are not overcrowded.

Fruit trees growing in grass often make little growth because they are starved of nitrogen. This can be remedied by feeding now with sulphate of ammonia or Nitrochalk, applied at the rate of about 4 oz. per tree. In cultivated soil, apples and pears will benefit from a dressing of sulphate of potash applied at the same rate and time, but such trees rarely need any extra nitrogen.

VEGETABLES

In the South and other sheltered areas and on light soils many seeds may now be sown under cloches. These include onions, carrots, peas, lettuces and radishes. The rows can be a little closer than they would be in the open, and in order still further to economise on space, carrots or peas can be sown down the centre with a row of let-

February: week 1

tuces or radishes on either side. These last will reach maturity and can be cleared well before the carrots or peas need extra space.

Lift and divide rhubarb clumps.

GREENHOUSE
Now is the time to bring the stools of outdoor chrysanthemums into the greenhouse and give them warmth and all the light possible so that they make sturdy growths from which cuttings can be taken.

In cold areas, broad beans and peas can be sown in pots now for planting out later on. Sow three or four peas in each 3½-in. pot, but only one bean per pot.

Cuttings of heliotrope which were inserted during the autumn should now be in 3½-in. pots on a shelf near the glass and making fresh growth. These young shoots will, in turn, be put in as cuttings for I find that spring-rooted cuttings make better plants for setting out in beds at the end of May. I like to plant them near a garden seat as they have a delightful scent on summer evenings. When rooted, pot the young plants singly into 3½-in. pots of John Innes No. 1 Potting Compost, and move them on into 5-in. pots as necessary. They are also good pot plants for the cool greenhouse.

If dahlias are to be raised from cuttings the tubers should be boxed up now and covered with moist peat. In a warm greenhouse they soon throw up plenty of shoots.

Spray fuchsias on warm, sunny days to encourage them to produce new shoots.

If the weather is mild and your greenhouse is warmed at night, schizanthus can be given a final move to 6- or 8-in. pots.

Cut back pelargoniums (geraniums), shortening the growths to within 6 to 9 in. of the pot. Then shake away the old soil and repot them in the smallest pots which will take the roots comfortably. Use John Innes No. 1 Potting Compost.

FLOWERS

Established herbaceous plants which have not recently been lifted and divided will benefit from feeding. Spread rotted manure or compost around the plants or sprinkle about a tablespoonful of general fertiliser around each plant, and fork in lightly.

Scabiosa Clive Greaves and other varieties of Caucasian Scabious are among the best herbaceous plants to give a continuous supply of cut flowers throughout the summer and early autumn. I would certainly advise gardeners who have not tried them to order some now for spring planting. These plants love lime, and ground lime-stone should be worked into the soil before planting at the rate of 4 oz. to the square yard. The plants do not take too kindly to frequent transplanting, so I grow mine in three batches, lifting and dividing one batch each year.

Also excellent for cutting are the perennial rudbeckias or Coneflowers. A striking one is *Rudbeckia speciosa* (*R. newmanii*). This is 2 to 3 ft. tall and has deep yellow petals around a purplish-black centre. The splendid *R. sullivantii* Goldsturm, with orange-yellow blooms, is only 1½ ft. tall.

It is not only the herbaceous plants which give us cut flowers, there are numerous shrubs which are splendid for this purpose, including forsythia, lilac, *Spiraea arguta* (sometimes known as Bridal Wreath) and *Choisya ternata* (the Mexican Orange Blossom). Many hardy annuals sown under cloches now will provide such flowers in early summer. Those I would especially recommend are larkspur, cornflower, godetia, calendula and helichrysum. Sweet pea seeds sown under cloches now will provide flowers for late summer.

If lily bulbs were not available for planting in late autumn (see p. 132) do this job now.

FRUIT

As the buds on gooseberry bushes begin to swell, they will become more attractive to bullfinches and other birds

February: week 2

They can be protected in various ways; for example, with a permanent fruit cage, or by covering the fruit bushes temporarily with fish netting, or by straining black thread from branch to branch over the bushes. I find that spraying with bird repellent also helps, but it must be repeated frequently.

The planting of fruit trees and bushes must be completed as soon as possible, before they start into growth.

Tar oil and DNOC winter washes must not be used on fruit once the buds begin to burst, though DNOC washes can be used with safety a little later than tar oil. If, for some reason, the time is missed for either of these sprayings it is still possible to use thiocyanate on the trees until well into March.

VEGETABLES
In the South and in other sheltered areas where the soil is not heavy, shallots can be planted. Space the bulbs 6 to 9 in. apart in rows 12 in. apart, and barely cover them with soil. Later, they will work their way to the surface.

After frost, look over the spring cabbages, and firm any that have been loosened by movement of the soil. This is also a good time to feed the plants with a quick-acting nitrogenous fertiliser such as nitrate of soda. It will serve as a tonic and help to increase the rate of growth as the days begin to lengthen.

Herbs such as sage and thyme which have become too large can be divided by pulling the clumps apart to provide small pieces with roots attached for replanting. In some cold districts the tops of sage plants may be damaged by frost in a hard winter. If this happens, the bushes should be cut down to within 9 in. of the ground and plenty of young shoots will then grow up from the base. In fact, all established sage and thyme bushes will benefit from this treatment which will ensure that there is a continual supply of young shoots.

February: week 2

GREENHOUSE

On bright days the temperature of the greenhouse may rise rapidly, so more attention must now be paid to ventilation. On sunny days most plants will benefit from a light overhead spray with clear water during the early part of the day.

A sowing of sweet peas made now in the greenhouse will provide plants for flowering in the late summer.

Other seeds to sow are *Asparagus sprengeri* and *A. plumosus*. A temperature of 18°C. (65°F.) is needed and the resulting seedlings should be potted singly in 3-in. pots using John Innes No. 1 Potting Compost. Move them on later to 5- or 6-in. pots. Seeds of these asparagus may be sown also in summer and autumn.

Cuttings of indoor chrysanthemums taken last month (see page 17) should be well rooted and ready for potting up separately. Use 3-in. pots and the John Innes No. 1 Potting Compost. Afterwards, encourage sturdy growth by maintaining a temperature of 7°C. (45°F.).

Protecting a gooseberry bush from bird damage by covering with netting

February: week 3

FLOWERS

Now is the time to fill any gaps in the wallflower bed before the plants begin to grow more actively. At the same time firm around those already planted as some may have been loosened by frost.

Plant lily-of-the-valley crowns before growth starts. The roots should be spread out in wide, shallow holes and covered with about 1 in. of soil. Established plants can be topdressed with compost or manure and fed with bonemeal at the rate of 4 oz. to the square yard.

Crocosmias – what we used to call montbretias – are often neglected and left to form such large clumps that they cannot give a good display of flowers. The newer varieties deteriorate very quickly under such conditions. Flowers will be of better quality and more numerous if the plants are divided every second year, and remember that some of the newer varieties are not completely hardy.

At this time of year I often remove old and poor shrubs and replace them with new specimens. Among my choices might well be the 4-ft. *Berberis thunbergii* which bears pale yellow flowers in spring and scarlet berries and brilliant red foliage in the autumn. Others to consider are the red-barked Dogwood, *Cornus alba*, which is such a cheerful sight in winter; and a winter-flowering viburnum like the fragrant, white, tinted pale pink *V. fragrans*, or the white-flowered *V. tinus*.

Correct planting is especially important with permanent subjects like shrubs. The soil must be suitable and the hole should be large enough to accommodate the roots at their full spread. So far as the planting depth is concerned, it is best to be guided by the soil mark on the stem for this will indicate the depth at which the plant was growing previously in the nursery. Before actually planting, cut off cleanly with sharp secateurs any broken or damaged roots.

In the South, the purple-flowered *Buddleia davidii* and its varieties should be pruned. (In other areas, wait until the end of March.) This is a shrub which it pays to prune severely, and the branches can be cut back to within $1\frac{1}{2}$ to 2 ft. of ground level. A feed with a general fertiliser after pruning will be beneficial.

FRUIT

In the warmer parts of the country the first flowers will now be showing on apricots, peaches and nectarines trained against sheltered walls. These should be protected against night frost with two or three thicknesses of garden netting or net curtains draped over the trees. Even better is hessian, which must be rolled back by day to admit light and allow the flowers to be pollinated.

Autumn-fruiting raspberries must be pruned now, all canes being cut back practically to ground level.

VEGETABLES

Watch out for slug damage under cloches, and use slug bait if necessary.

Plant out autumn-sown onions spacing them 9 in. apart in rows 15 in. apart. The ground should be well dug and manured, in an open position.

Preparing fuchsia cuttings. 1. A clean cut should be made just below a leaf joint. 2. After dipping in rooting powder the cuttings are inserted around the edge of a 3-in. pot

February: week 3

Continue to plant shallots. These like an open site with deeply dug soil and good drainage, and although the soil needs to contain plenty of plant food it should not have been recently manured. For further details see p. 28.

A similar site is needed by garlic, but the soil need not be quite so rich as for shallots. Plant the bulbs 2 in. deep and 6 in. apart in rows 8 in. apart. This is a useful plant to grow between other crops.

Round-seeded peas can be sown now in a sheltered border. All peas like a well-prepared and well-manured soil.

One third of the vegetable garden should be limed each year before the end of February. Apply hydrated lime at the rate of 4 to 6 oz. to the square yard – but not when potatoes are to be planted for this encourages scab.

GREENHOUSE

Early onion seedlings should be pricked out into boxes of John Innes No. 1 Potting Compost spacing them 3 in. apart each way.

Fuchsia cuttings taken now will root quickly in a warm propagator and make good plants for greenhouse decoration or for planting out at the end of May. Use hormone rooting powder and insert them in sandy compost.

Two verbenas which I value greatly for use in hanging baskets and window-boxes, for bedding and for growing as specimens in pots are the bright scarlet Lawrence Johnston and the pale blue Loveliness. I keep a few plants of each for stock, and hundreds of cuttings can be obtained from the growths on these and rooted during the spring.

Lupins and delphiniums can be grown from seed sown in the greenhouse now. Such plants will come into flower in August or September and will be very vigorous.

Continue to pot up cuttings of indoor chrysanthemums as they become sufficiently rooted (see p. 29).

February: week 4

FLOWERS

If the weather is mild, the spring flowers will already be opening. In my Shropshire garden the snowdrops are often out by the middle of January. *Primula* Wanda is another early gem and some of the other primulas, such as *P. rosea* and *P. denticulata* and the common primrose (*P. vulgaris*), show their first flowers at this time.

One of the best late-summer shrubs is the creamy-flowered *Hydrangea paniculata*. To encourage strong growth carrying large panicles of bloom, prune hard back now in a similar way to the purple buddleia I referred to last week.

Shrubs such as the Common Dogwood and the red-and yellow-twigged willows which are grown for the colour of their young stems are also best pruned hard back each year to encourage strong young growth. The prunings can be used as hard-wood cuttings, and if inserted outdoors in a sheltered place they will soon form roots.

If roses were attacked by black spot in previous years, remove and burn any dead leaves from the soil around the plants and then spray with a copper fungicide to kill the resting spores. A spray consisting of 1 oz. copper sulphate to 1 gallon of water can be made up and the plants and the soil beneath them duly treated.

Already lawn grass will be showing signs of new growth, and it will not be long before the mowing season is back again. Rake or sweep the lawn to scatter worm casts if this was not done last month.

FRUIT

If gooseberries were not pruned earlier for fear of bird damage, this should be done now. Bushes should be shaped as they are pruned and generally only a light thinning is necessary after dead, diseased and crossing branches have been removed. Trained gooseberries should be spur pruned, that is, all young side growths should be cut back to two or three buds.

February: week 4

Fig trees on outside walls can also be pruned. Cut out some of the old wood and train in the long, young branches. Make sure that the fan shape is maintained.

Currant and gooseberry cuttings put in last autumn may need firming if they have been lifted by frost.

Spray outdoor peaches and nectarines with a copper fungicide as a protection against leaf curl.

VEGETABLES

Chives are a useful substitute for spring onions in a salad and now is a good time to divide and replant them. They like any ordinary soil and a sunny position.

In a sheltered border you can now sow Brussels sprouts and early cabbages as well as making a first sowing of leeks.

Lettuces and radishes can also be sown when the weather is favourable and the soil dry enough to form a good seed bed.

Radishes are often sown between rows of Brussels sprouts and broad beans as they are quick to mature and a useful catch crop. Make the drills about $\frac{1}{2}$ in. deep and sow thinly, pulling the roots as required.

GREENHOUSE

Freesias which finished flowering some weeks ago can now be laid on their sides in their pots to dry off.

Small, scaly tubers of achimenes should be removed from the dry soil in which they have overwintered and a few may be potted for early flowering. Start them into growth in a mixture of moist peat and sand. Push them into the compost and give a temperature of 13 to 16°C. (55 to 60°F.) to encourage growth to start. When the young shoots appear pot them up into 5- or 6-in. pots, spacing the plants 2 to 3 in. apart. Use the John Innes No. 1 Potting Compost.

Seeds of antirrhinums, salvias, ageratums, lobelias and petunias may be sown but leave other half-hardy annuals – such as French and African marigolds, annual phlox, stocks and asters – until the end of March or early April.

Seeds of tuberous begonias and gloxinias sown now will provide flowering plants by mid-summer. Cover the very small seeds with sand rather than compost and germinate in a propagating frame with a temperature of 18 to 21°C. (65 to 70°F.). Sow seed, too, of *Begonia semperflorens* and germinate at 16°C. (60°F.).

Young shoots on Lorraine begonias kept in warm conditions can now be used for cuttings. Trim the base of each cutting just below a leaf joint with a sharp knife and root several cuttings round the edge of a 3-in. pot in a propagator with a temperature of 18°C. (65°F.).

Young shoots on vines should be reduced to one or two per spur. When the shoots are 2 to 3 in. long the rods, which were lowered in December (see p. 152), should be tied back in position against the side of the greenhouse.

If clivias have not been repotted for several years this can be done now, but over-potting is something to be avoided. Use the John Innes No. 1 Potting Compost, and if new plants are wanted, the crowns can be divided at this stage.

As schizanthus become well established in their final pots, feed them once a fortnight with weak liquid manure. All feeding of pot plants should be done sparingly. Fertiliser should never be given to pot plants when the soil is dry or the roots will be scorched; first water and then apply the fertiliser. Most plants which have begun to make growth can also be fed once a fortnight.

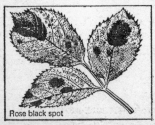

Rose black spot

Peach leaf curl

March: week 1

FLOWERS

Keep a pair of secateurs handy for there are a number of shrubs which need pruning now, including the late-flowering *Caryopteris clandonensis*. All last year's flowering branches should be cut back to about an inch.

Unlike so many other bulbous-rooted plants, snow-drops can be lifted and divided as soon as the flowers fade. There is no advantage in waiting until the foliage has died down. It is advisable to lift and replant in this way every few years to prevent overcrowding.

Oil and grease the lawn mower ready for the mowing season which will soon be starting. Make sure that the blades are really sharp and correctly adjusted.

Herbaceous perennials may be planted now. Always plan your borders before you begin planting, and plant in groups so that you obtain the maximum colour effect.

If Brompton stocks have been overwintered in a cold frame they should be bedded out now.

This is a good time to plant the corms of the lovely autumn-flowering *Cyclamen neapolitanum*. These grow particularly well under a beech or oak tree for they like cool, shady conditions.

FRUIT

Peach, nectarine and apricot trees growing on walls will now be in flower in many parts of the country. If the weather is cold and windy, there will be few insects air-borne to pollinate the flowers, so use a fine paint brush to hand pollinate them.

There is still time to spray apple and pear trees with thiocyanate winter wash if tar oil or DNOC washes were not used during January or February.

If fruit trees have been ordered make quite sure that the site for them has been prepared. Nothing is more harmful to trees and bushes at this time of year than getting their roots dry, so even if you cannot plant them take off the straw wrappings, soak the roots and cover these with soil or wet sacks until planting can be carried out.

VEGETABLES

In the southern counties and in many parts of the Midlands sowing in the vegetable garden can now begin in earnest. The preparation of the seed bed itself is an important job. If the soil was dug over during the winter and left rough to expose as much of the area as possible to frost, it should crumble down easily and there should be little difficulty in obtaining the fine tilth which is the hallmark of a good seed bed. It is important to tread the bed well and to make certain that it is firm all over. Finish off by raking to provide a fine, level surface.

First sowings of onions, parsnips and broad beans may now be made. Sow the onion seed in drills 1 ft. apart. Later the plants will be thinned to about 6 in. apart in the rows. In the case of parsnips drop three or four seeds into the drill at intervals of 9 to 12 in. and thin out later. Sow broad beans in drills 3 in. deep and 2 ft. apart and set the seeds 4 to 6 in. apart in the rows.

Jerusalem artichokes are useful plants for screening the compost heap or garden shed and their 6-ft. tall stems will also make a good windbreak in an exposed garden. Sometimes they produce large, yellow, sunflower-like blooms which are an added attraction. Plant the tubers

Hand pollinating peach blossom with the aid of a camel-hair brush to ensure a good crop of fruit

15 in. apart and 3 in. deep in rows 3 ft. apart. They will grow almost anywhere, and are especially suitable in soil that is not rich enough for potatoes.

GREENHOUSE

Schizanthus plants will need stopping again to encourage a branching habit. This also applies to the fuchsias which were pruned earlier and are now making several growths.

The sun will be gaining warmth and on bright days it will be necessary to damp the pots and staging and to spray growing plants overhead. This will provide the moist atmospheric conditions that plants need if they are to flourish.

If coleus plants are to be grown from seed, this can be sown now. Germinate in a propagating frame with a temperature of 16 to 18°C. (60 to 65°F.).

Dahlia cuttings can be prepared as well as soft-wood cuttings of many other plants including coleus, heliotrope and verbena. All will root readily in a sandy compost in a warm propagating frame.

A few tubers of begonias and gloxinias should now be started into growth. Press them into boxes of moist peat and sand, and grow them on in a moist atmosphere.

Young plants of indoor chrysanthemums in 3-in. pots may now be moved to a frame. It is an advantage if the frame is heated, but if not it must be covered on cold nights with straw or sacking. Watch the watering carefully, and if the weather turns cold keep the soil rather dry.

It is best to raise new plants of *Solanum capsicastrum* from seed annually. A temperature of 16 to 18°C. (60 to 65°F.) is needed for germination.

Sow Brussels sprout seed in a frame or cool greenhouse.

Now is the time to take cuttings of outdoor chrysanthemums. They should be rooted in exactly the same way as those of indoor varieties.

FLOWERS

During the next few weeks hardy annuals of all kinds should be sown where they are to flower. Later on the seedlings will have to be thinned out according to their type. The soil must be in ideal condition for sowing, that is, it should be drying on the surface and sufficiently crumbly to allow it to be raked down to a fine tilth.

Nasturtiums are one of the many hardy annuals which give such a colourful display during the summer. Sow the seed now, and remember that the double varieties are best as they do not seed themselves and become a nuisance. Dwarf Double Gleam is one to consider.

The new shoots of some of the earlier-flowering herbaceous plants are now ready for thinning. Generally they are reduced to between five and eight per clump.

Bulbs which have finished flowering indoors may either be tipped out of their bowls and heeled in or planted out between shrubs where they can grow permanently.

Large-flowered clematis, such as *Clematis jackmanii* and the many hybrids derived from it should be pruned at this time, and all are better for being cut back quite severely. I shorten mine to within 2 to $2\frac{1}{2}$ ft. of the ground each year, cutting back to good, well-developed buds.

Lawns should now be fed with a general organic-based fertiliser. Follow the manufacturer's instructions and spread evenly over the surface.

FRUIT

Where fruit trees have recently been planted in grass, be careful to keep a clean cultivated area of 2 to 3 ft. around the trunks. If this precaution is not taken the trees will suffer from lack of nitrogen and will make little new growth.

Plums and damsons will now be coming into flower in many gardens.

Feed raspberries, loganberries and blackberries with a

March: week 2

general organic-based garden fertiliser at the rate of 4 oz. to each plant. Keep the fertiliser away from the stems of the plants or they may be scorched.

A good general fertiliser can also be sprinkled between the rows of strawberries and around the plants, but again be careful to keep it off the leaves and crowns. While doing this, clean up the bed by picking off any dead leaves and then prick over the surface lightly with a fork.

VEGETABLES

In the South and in sheltered places it is worth the risk of planting a few early potatoes. It is possible that later on their first shoots may be cut by late frosts, but that is a chance worth taking. I am particularly fond of the old variety Sharpe's Express which may not be as heavy a cropper as some, but which does have an excellent flavour.

Prepare celery trenches making them 1½ ft. wide and 3 ft. apart. Do not make them so deep that the celery has to be planted in the cold subsoil. Break up the soil deeply, but leave the finished trench 6 to 8 in. below the surface. Work in plenty of well-rotted manure or compost, for celery likes plenty of moisture.

Broad beans and peas started in pots or boxes indoors should now be hardened off for planting out in a week or two's time.

Sow seeds now of summer and autumn cabbages such as Winningstadt and Primo.

GREENHOUSE

Pot on young cyclamen plants sown last June into 4-in. pots. Afterwards, they should be housed in a cool greenhouse.

Sweet peas which have been raised in the greenhouse should be hardened off.

Hydrangeas in pots should be fed from now on with weak liquid manure at 10- to 14-day intervals.

As soon as fuchsia cuttings have rooted pot them separately in 3-in. pots, using either John Innes No. 1 Potting Compost or a soilless compost. When the plants are about 6 in. tall, pinch out the growing tips to encourage the plants to make bushy growth.

Sow seed of pansies, violas and polyanthus.

Some cuttings of indoor chrysanthemums, already well rooted and potted, will be in need of their first stopping. For general decorative purposes, I stop all the mid-season varieties during the middle of March and again in the middle of June.

Bring pot-grown lilies which have been overwintered in a frame into the greenhouse. These had their pots only half filled with compost originally, and should now be topdressed with fresh compost to within $\frac{1}{2}$ in. of the rims. Start feeding them in a week or so with a liquid fertiliser and continue once a week until they show flower buds.

Sow tomato seed now. A minimum temperature of 16°C. (60°F.) is essential for good germination.

When sowing an annual border it is best to mark out the design first with a pointed stick. Seeds can then be allocated to each area, and, after sprinkling them lightly over the surface, they should be raked in

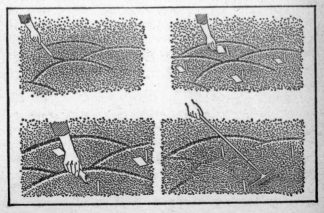

March: week 3

FLOWERS

I am sufficiently old-fashioned to believe that late March is the proper time to prune hybrid tea roses, despite what others may say about the advantages of winter pruning. If fine exhibition flowers are needed, prune severely, cutting all strong young growths back to three or four buds from the position where growth started last spring. For general garden purposes it is not necessary to prune so hard and good shoots may be left with five or six buds, only the weaker ones being cut back to two or three.

The floribundas can be pruned fairly lightly in a similar manner to hybrid teas being grown for garden display. Climbing roses on walls should have their side branches cut back to within two buds of the main stems. All newly planted hybrid teas and floribundas being pruned for the first time should be cut back to within 6 or 8 in. of the ground. This is important, as an initial hard pruning encourages strong growth the first year.

Where rose bushes have been neglected for several years and have acquired a lot of old wood, some drastic thinning may be needed, but do not expect to get good new growth from stumps of old hard wood. The best of the young growth should be retained and shortened.

After pruning, spray the bushes against black spot. If this disease has been troublesome scrape off the top $\frac{1}{2}$ in. of soil and replace this with fresh soil or peat. Then feed the roses with bonemeal applied at the rate of a handful per bush or with a fertiliser having a fairly high phosphate content. Alternatively, one of the special rose fertilisers may be used.

Plant gladiolus corms for early flowering. Spread the planting period over the next six weeks to provide continuity. The corms should be planted 3 to 4 in. deep. On heavy soils put a layer of sand at the bottom of each hole to improve drainge and lessen the possibility of the corms rotting.

Remove the panes of glass which were placed over choice alpines for protection last autumn.

FRUIT

This is the time to mulch wall-trained fruit trees and all newly planted fruit trees with compost, very strawy manure or even straw. On no account use wet, sticky manure for this purpose.

Where trees are planted against a wall, remember that the soil here often becomes very dry, so water freely when necessary.

Spray black currants with malathion against big bud mite when the most forward of the young leaves are about an inch across.

VEGETABLES

As soon as soil conditions allow sow maincrop leeks. If necessary use cloches to get the soil sufficiently dry.

In sheltered borders or where the soil is light, stump-rooted carrots can be sown now. Continue to do so at intervals throughout the season as a catch crop.

Pelleted seeds are becoming increasingly available and their great advantage is that they make accurate placement very easy, thus cutting down the need for thinning. Particularly useful in pelleted form are carrots and lettuces.

Supporting the flowering stems of a calceolaria. The canes should slope outwards to open up the growth of the plant

March: week 3

Give winter lettuces a little general fertiliser to hurry their growth along, but be very careful to keep this off the leaves. Do not use more than 2 oz. to each yard of row and hoe it in afterwards.

GREENHOUSE

Annuals sown during the autumn for flowering in pots are now growing rapidly and will benefit from weekly feeding.

Staking and tying needs attention, in particular with salpiglossis, clarkias, schizanthus and calceolarias.

If a temperature of 16°C. (60°F.) is available at night, sow seeds of verbena, nicotiana and thunbergia. Freesias, too, can be sown but they need 18°C. (65°F.).

Young perlargoniums (geraniums) should be moved on into 5- or 6-in. pots. When the plants are 6 to 8 in. tall pinch out the tips of the shoots to encourage a bushy habit.

As soon as perpetual-flowering carnations fill their pots they should be moved on into 5-in. pots, using the John Innes No. 1 Potting Compost. Keep the plants in a cool, light, airy place. When eight pairs of leaves have developed the tips should be pulled out to encourage side-shoots to develop.

Ferns can be repotted now and started into growth by placing them at the warm end of the greenhouse. If the plants are becoming quite large they can be divided.

Asparagus ferns, *Asparagus plumosus* and *A. sprengeri*, can also be divided by cutting the growths apart with a sharp knife. Pot each piece in a 5-in. pot using John Innes No. 1 Potting Compost.

As the cuttings of outdoor chrysanthemums develop a good root system, they should be potted up singly in 3-in. pots of John Innes No. 1 Potting Compost. Give them cool, light conditions so that growth is sturdy.

FLOWERS

Pansies or violas can now be sown out of doors in a nursery bed. They will be sufficiently mature to flower during the late summer and again next year and are excellent as an edging to rose beds.

The popular Japonica (*Chaenomeles speciosa*) is one of those shrubs which should be pruned when flowering has finished. When grown as a bush in the open it requires little or no pruning, but if it is planted as a wall shrub it is necessary to keep it in shape.

The fragrant *Daphne mezereum* is a spring-flowering shrub which should not be pruned as it dislikes cutting of any kind. This shrub has a life span of about eight to ten years and then has to be replaced. It does not like root disturbance, so young pot-grown specimens should be bought.

Penstemons overwintering in frames should be given full ventilation now.

Autumn-sown annuals may need thinning and after this twiggy sticks can be put around them for support.

In mild places sweet peas can be sown out of doors.

FRUIT

In cool districts where pears are not yet in flower they should be given their pre-blossom spraying with lime sulphur or captan as a preventive for scab. Derris or BHC may be given with either of these sprays if there is any suspicion that caterpillars or aphids are active.

VEGETABLES

Plant more potatoes, giving preference to early varieties.

This is a good time to start new mint beds or to replant old ones. This should be done every two years to reduce the possibility of rust. Mint is very vigorous, so restrict the roots within the confines of an old bucket or sink.

Make the first outdoor sowing of wrinkled or marrowfat peas. I make a drill the full width of a spade and $1\frac{1}{2}$ in. deep and space three rows of peas in this. The

March: week 4

seeds themselves are spaced 2 to 3 in. apart. Varieties which will grow 18 in. to 2 ft. tall should be grown in rows at least 2 ft. apart. Varieties which will grow 3 to 4 ft. tall should have that distance left between the rows. While the pea plants are still young, the space between can be used to grow a catch crop of radishes, lettuces or spinach.

Make a sowing of turnips on fairly rich, but not newly manured ground.

Where rhubarb is being forced, take the covers off now or the plants will become very weak.

If onions are to be grown from sets, these can be planted now. I prefer to plant them just below the surface using a trowel rather than a dibber. I find that there is then less likelihood of the sets pushing themselves out of the ground as they grow.

GREENHOUSE

Seedlings must be pricked out before they become too crowded. It is often difficult to find space for all the boxes and a shelf near the glass can prove very useful.

Sow seeds of *Primula obconica* and *P. sinensis* and give them a temperature of 16°C. (60°F.).

Insert coleus cuttings in sandy compost in a propagating frame with a temperature of 16°C. (60°F.). It is best to take the cuttings in batches so that there is a continuity of young plants for these have the best colour.

Young coleus plants raised from seed should be ready for pricking out singly into 3-in. pots filled with John Innes No. 1 Potting Compost.

Half-hardy annuals to sow now include French and African marigolds, annual phlox, asters, celosias, nemesias, salpiglossis, ten-week stocks and zinnias.

Start tubers of pendulous begonias in a mixture of peat and sand. These plants are particularly attractive in hanging baskets.

Prick out seedlings of *Begonia semperflorens* into boxes of John Innes No. 1 Potting Compost.

March: week 4

Start a few more begonia and gloxinia tubers. The begonias can be bedded out when all fear of frost has passed.

Tuberous begonias and gloxinias started earlier should now be ready for potting. Put the begonias into 5-in. pots and use John Innes No. 2 Potting Compost. Place the tubers halfway down the pots and cover them with about ½ in. of compost. When established, topdress with more compost so that the tubers are 2 in. below the surface.

Gloxinias are treated in a similar way except that no space is left for topdressing and the tubers are covered with about 1 in. of soil.

Cuttings of winter-flowering begonias taken in February should be potted into 3-in. pots of John Innes No. 1 Potting Compost and given a temperature of 16 to 18°C. (60 to 65°F.).

When the sun comes out the temperature inside the greenhouse rises rapidly so the ventilators must be used, a little at a time at first and always on the sheltered side of the house. They should be closed again before the sun goes down.

Late-flowering chrysanthemums should be given their first stopping. The second one will be towards the end of June.

Before planting potato tubers the surplus shoots should be rubbed away, leaving only the two or three strongest

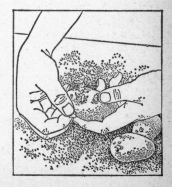

April: week 1

FLOWERS
Some choice herbaceous plants can be propagated from
cuttings taken now. This is true of delphiniums, herbaceous phlox, lupins and heleniums. All will grow well
from young shoots cut off below ground level, close to
the crown of the plant. With delphiniums and lupins it is
particularly important to get well down, because higher
up the growth is hollow and will not root easily. Dip the
ends of the cuttings in a rooting powder and insert them
in a cold frame. Water them well, cover the frame with
glass and shade from bright sunshine.

Lawns now need regular mowing, and the edges must
be kept neatly trimmed. If this job is done fairly frequently before the grass gets too long there will be no
need to pick up the clippings as they will soon wither and
mix with the soil.

The South African chincherinchee, *Ornithogalum thyr-
soides*, makes a first-class cut flower as well as a valuable
garden plant. The white blooms, marked brownish-green
at the centre, are borne on 2-ft. stems and the narrow
leaves are about half this length. It is not usually hardy
and the bulbs should be lifted in October, stored in a cool,
dry place and replanted at this time of year. I make a
trench for the bulbs some 4 to 5 in. deep and sprinkle
sand along its base. The bulbs are then spaced 2 to 3 in.
apart and covered with soil. The site chosen must be
sunny and the soil well drained if they are to do really
well. The flowers are borne in late July, August and September.

FRUIT
It is always worth while pollinating wall-grown fruit trees
by hand as they come into full flower. This can be done
by jarring the tree or by dusting the open flowers with a
rabbit's tail or camel-hair brush.

Watch peaches and nectarines for any sign of aphids
on the young leaves, and spray with BHC if they do
appear, before the leaves curl and give the insects pro-

tection. If necessary, a fungicide such as lime sulphur can be added to protect against mildew and leaf curl.

If black currants have not already been sprayed, this should be done now with malathion as, except in the coldest localities, this is the latest time for it to be effective against the big bud mite.

Mulch between the rows of raspberries, blackberries and loganberries with well-rotted manure, compost or peat. This will keep the roots moist as well as feed the plants.

VEGETABLES

Brussels sprouts sown earlier in a frame or greenhouse should now be pricked out in the open ground. Space them 4 to 6 in. apart so that they have room to develop sturdily. Early plants are the ones which produce the finest crops.

Complete the planting of early potatoes and start on the maincrop varieties, particularly if you live in the South or West. Good varieties include Pentland Crown, Majestic and Arran Banner.

Spring cabbages should be given a light topdressing with a general fertiliser to hurry along growth. Such a dressing should always be hoed in.

Early sowings of many vegetables under cloches may

Dipping lupin cuttings in hormone rooting powder before inserting them in a sandy compost

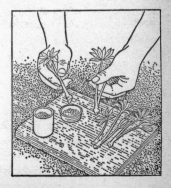

April: week 1

need thinning, otherwise the plants will be weak and spindly.

Seedlings of broad beans and peas which have been gradually hardened off during the last few weeks should now be in a suitable condition to plant out.

Parsley seed can be sown now for summer use. This is often very slow to germinate, so do not be surprised if several weeks elapse before the seedlings appear.

GREENHOUSE
The sowing of half-hardy annuals should be completed this week. Many seedlings from earlier sowings will be in need of pricking out and some of the most forward may even need to be potted individually.

It is also time to sow seed of outdoor tomatoes. Bush tomatoes, like Amateur, are particularly useful for this purpose. Tomato plants to be grown in a moderately heated greenhouse should be ready for pricking out now into 3½-in. pots filled with John Innes No. 1 Potting Compost. They need a temperature of 16°C. (60°F.) to maintain satisfactory growth.

Sow seeds of *Mimosa pudica*, the Sensitive Plant. This plant is quite a novelty with its sensitive leaves which close up at the slightest touch. The resulting plants will be ready for potting up in late May.

Grevillea and jacaranda are two other plants grown in the greenhouse for their foliage effects, and seeds should be sown now.

Prick out seedlings of tuberous begonias and gloxinias into boxes filled with John Innes No. 1 Potting Compost, and provide them with shady conditions and a temperature of 18°C. (65°F.).

Sow seed of celery and celeriac in the greenhouse now to provide plants for planting out in prepared trenches in June. Celeriac is a useful vegetable for flavouring soups and stews. It forms turnip-like roots which are lifted in the autumn and stored until required.

FLOWERS

This is a good time of year to make a new lawn from seed. Watch the weather and sow the grass seed as soon as the soil is in a reasonably dry, crumbly condition. A really good seed bed must be prepared, and time spent on levelling, firming and raking is well worth the effort. The grass seed should be broadcast as evenly as possible over the surface and then raked in. If black cotton can be stretched over the ground it will help to keep the birds away.

It is most important to purchase good grass seed which does not contain too much rye grass. Nowadays, mixtures are available for special purposes to provide top-quality lawns, hard-wearing lawns, lawns for shade and so on. A suitable rate of sowing is $1\frac{1}{2}$ oz. to the square yard. Some seed is treated with a bird repellent dressing.

This is the time to plant sweet pea seedlings. They can be planted either in single rows or in double rows 9 in. apart with 9 in. between the plants. For really good cut flowers it is best to grow the plants on single stems, selecting the strongest shoot from the base of each plant and removing all sideshoots throughout the growing season. Long canes should be used to support the plants and a sturdy framework should be made to resist the wind.

There is still time to sow all kinds of hardy annuals, but the sooner this is done the better.

As forsythias finish flowering they should be pruned. The way to do this is to cut out the stems which have just flowered but to keep all young stems, as it is these which will bear the best flowers next year.

Clematis should be planted now, and it is best, if possible, to obtain pot-grown plants.

Continue to plant gladiolus corms.

FRUIT

Disbudding of peaches, nectarines and apricots can begin. With fan-trained trees rub out all shoots which are growing on the backs of the branches – towards the wall – and the fronts of the branches – away from the wall. The best to retain are those on the tops of the branches.

Put cloches over strawberries to encourage the ripening of a few early fruits.

Spray gooseberries against mildew with lime sulphur or with a washing soda spray on sulphur-shy varieties such as Leveller.

VEGETABLES

Sowings of lettuces, carrots, radishes and peas should continue. A good maincrop variety of carrot is James's Scarlet Intermediate. Among lettuces, the cos type are much to be valued; a favourite variety is Little Gem. Continue to sow for succession until August. French Breakfast and Cherry Belle are good varieties of radish, and Kelvedon Wonder and Onward are popular peas.

Early-sown peas which have already germinated will be helped if the soil is drawn up a little on either side of each row. Similarly with broad beans.

It is too early to sow French beans without any protection except in the mildest localities, but in most places they can be sown with safety under cloches.

In the South sow a little round beetroot seed for an early crop. Do not sow too much as the beet soon becomes coarse; it is much better to make successional sowings from early April until July to give a continuous supply of young beets.

Winter greens such as the ordinary winter cabbage January King, savoy cabbage and broccoli (both the heading and sprouting kinds) should all be sown now.

GREENHOUSE

Remember that a slightly humid atmosphere is essential in houses where nectarines and peaches are growing. This is achieved mainly by early morning syringing and damping down the floors. If the weather is sunny, damp down again at mid-day. Dry air would encourage the development of both thrips and red spider.

Sow seeds of both melons and cucumbers. The best method is to place two seeds in each 3-in. pot, and if both seeds germinate, reduce them to one. Germinate in a temperature of 18 to 21°C. (65 to 70°F.). Cantaloupe melons are a good choice for they have a fine flavour and are excellent under glass.

As pot-grown camellias finish flowering, they can be repotted into larger pots if those in which they are at present growing are well filled with roots. Use a special camellia compost consisting of 2 parts peat, 1 part lime-free loam and 1 part coarse sand.

Greenhouse chrysanthemums, now housed in frames, will need potting on into 5-in. pots using John Innes No. 2 Potting Compost. As the plants become established, leave the lights off during the day.

Vine rods growing in unheated greenhouses should be tied up to their supporting wires as growth should be sufficiently well advanced all along the rods.

Young plants of outdoor chrysanthemums should be moved to a cold frame and hardened off gradually.

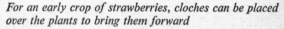

For an early crop of strawberries, cloches can be placed over the plants to bring them forward

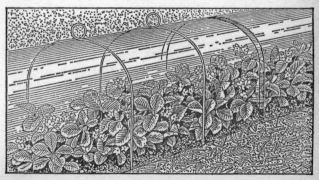

April: week 3

FLOWERS

It will soon be time to plant border chrysanthemums outside and it is most important that the soil should be well
prepared. Space the plants at least $1\frac{1}{2}$ ft. apart and allow
2 ft. between the rows so that there is sufficient room to
work between them when weeding, stopping, disbudding
and so on. I always put the canes or stakes in position
first and plant to these, tying the plants in immediately.

As daffodils and other bulbs finish blooming, remove
the dead flowers. This keeps the garden tidy and also pre-
vents seed formation and encourages the bulbs to grow.

It is also wise to pick dead flowers of pansies and violas
regularly before they produce any seed pods. Greenfly
often makes a first appearance on these plants and on
polyanthus, so as soon as it is seen spray with a BHC insecticide.

Take advantage of any fine, mild weather to harden off
the more tender summer bedding plants that cannot, with
safety, be planted out until well on in May. A frame is the
best place for these now, and on really good spring-like
days the lights can be removed altogether for a few
hours.

Young penstemon plants overwintering in frames
should be stopped by pinching out their growing tips.
This will encourage them to form bushy, well-shaped
plants.

Cuttings of rhododendrons and azaleas are not easy to
root, but these plants can be readily increased by layers.
Choose branches of last year's growth which can be bent
down easily to soil level and make a slit halfway through
the stem and on the lower side where it touches the soil.
Dust this wounded portion with hormone rooting
powder and peg it firmly to the ground. A mixture of peat
and sand added to the soil at this point will facilitate
rooting.

If hebes (which used to be known as veronicas) have
been damaged by severe frost they can be cut back hard
now.

FRUIT

Raspberries should be sprayed for the first time with derris as a precaution against the raspberry beetle. If mildew was troublesome last year, add a colloidal copper fungicide to the insecticide.

If the weather should turn dry, make sure that newly planted fruit trees and bushes are not short of water while they are becoming established.

When apple blossom reaches the pink bud stage, which is just before the buds open fully, spray with lime sulphur or captan as a precaution against scab and add BHC to kill any caterpillars or greenfly that may be about.

VEGETABLES

Parsnips raised from seed sown last month will now be ready for thinning, if the weather has been favourable. Thin the seedlings to at least 9 in. apart in the rows.

As soon as the rows of onions and carrots can be seen clearly hoe between them, both to aerate the soil and destroy any weeds. As it is after hoeing that these plants are most likely to be attacked by onion fly and carrot fly, dust along the rows with BHC. Brassica seedlings should be dusted occasionally with BHC to kill flea beetles.

Maincrop potatoes should be planted now. Give them plenty of room and plant in narrow trenches chopped out

Dusting brassica seedlings with BHC powder as a protection against flea beetle, an insect which eats holes in the leaves

with a spade. If the seed potatoes have been sprouting, reduce the growths to the three best on each tuber.

Prepare trenches for runner beans to be sown or planted next month by digging the soil thoroughly and incorporating plenty of well-rotted manure or garden compost. I sometimes recommend sowing the seeds in pots, one seed to each 3-in. pot. They can then be germinated in a greenhouse, frame or even under cloches and the resulting seedlings transplanted to their growing positions at the end of May.

Onion plants which were raised from seeds sown in the greenhouse last December, can now be planted out.

GREENHOUSE
More achimenes can be started, and begonias and gloxinias started a few weeks ago should be ready for potting up.

Standard fuchsias should be stopped for the last time. Young plants being grown to form new standards should now have reached the required height for the head of branches to be developed. This is done by pinching out the central growing tip to encourage sideshoots to form.

Make up hanging baskets with pelargoniums, lobelia, verbena and other trailing plants. I particularly like pendulous fuchsias for this purpose. The baskets should be lined with moss and John Innes No. 3 Potting Compost is placed around the roots of the plants.

Stake pot-grown lilies, taking care not to damage the bulbs when inserting the canes.

Solanum seedlings should be pricked out into 3-in. pots filled with John Innes No. 1 Potting Compost.

Early-planted tomatoes will be in need of side-shooting. This means that all the side growths forming in the axils of the leaves are removed. Water carefully until the first fruits have formed, and from then onwards feed the plants weekly with a good tomato fertiliser.

Tie vine growths to the training wires as necessary.

FLOWERS

Dahlia tubers can be planted now with safety, but plant them reasonably deeply to prevent frost damage. The tubers can be divided up at this time, provided there is a piece of stem attached to each tuber. If new shoots have started to develop, do not plant until the end of May or the beginning of June as frost could damage the young growths.

Penstemons and half-hardy calceolarias which have been overwintering in a frame may also be planted out now.

Spot treatment of weeds in lawns can begin. This method can even be carried out between shrubs and other plants as long as the selective weedkiller is not allowed to blow onto them.

Water lilies and all other kinds of hardy aquatics can be planted during the next few weeks.

In sheltered areas, sow seeds of statice, helichrysum and acroclinium. These can be cut and dried in August for use in flower arrangements. In cold districts they are better sown under glass in March.

FRUIT

If some strawberry plants are to be used to give early runners for propagation purposes, they should not be

Unwanted shoots on wall-trained peaches and apricots must be removed regularly if the trees are to be kept under control

April: week 4

allowed to flower. Make certain that any plants reserved for this purpose look really healthy with no yellow mottling or rolling of the leaves which might indicate virus.

Strawberries which are to be allowed to flower and fruit should be protected from late frost. Newspapers placed over them on cold nights still make quite a difference, or straw may be kept at hand to be sprinkled lightly over the plants on any evening when there appears to be a threat of frost. It is most important to watch plum trees for the first sign of aphid attack, spraying at once if this pest is seen.

Complete the disbudding of wall-trained peaches, nectarines and apricots. Again, keep a look out for insect attack.

VEGETABLES
Complete the planting of maincrop potatoes and earth up any early ones which are showing through the soil to protect them against night frosts.

Put up the supports for runner beans, using either sticks or string. A seedling can then be planted against each support or the seed sown direct in the ground.

If celery trenches have not already been prepared (see p. 40), complete this work as soon as possible.

Sow sweet corn and marrow seeds in 3-in. pots and place these in a garden frame. The bush type of marrow is best for the average garden as it is less spreading than the trailing kind. Varieties include Green Bush, White Bush and Superlative. Courgettes are also very good and are treated in the same way.

GREENHOUSE
Many half-hardy annuals will now be ready for pricking out. Some are better if pricked out straight into pots rather than trays in which they are apt to get starved.

This is also the time to prick out tomato seedlings which will be planted out of doors after hardening off.

Young growths of vines should be pinched back to two

leaves beyond the fruit trusses, and if two bunches of fruit form on one lateral, one should be removed. Secondary growths which develop should have their tips taken out at one leaf, and tendrils should be removed.

Fuchsias must now be moved on into larger pots. Use the 5-in. size and John Innes No. 2 Potting Compost.

Seedlings of *Begonia semperflorens* should now be potted into 3-in. pots. They will be planted outside in June.

Pendulous begonias which were started into growth at the end of March should now be planted into their hanging baskets. These flowers are ideal for a shady position in the sun lounge or conservatory.

Prick out pansies and violas into boxes and pot up coleus cuttings in 3-in. pots.

Dracaenas, codiaeums and rubber plants (*Ficus elastica*) which have grown too much may be reduced in size by air layering. An inch-long cut is made half way through the stem at a convenient point, and this wounded area is treated with hormone rooting powder, covered with damp moss and, finally, sealed with polythene. When roots have formed in the moss the stem can be severed just below the point of layering, the polythene removed and the new plant potted up. Do not remove the moss or the roots may be damaged.

Spot treatment of a lawn weed by painting herbicide directly onto the plant. This is most effective with persistent weeds

May: week 1

FLOWERS

Many half-hardy bedding plants will be offered for sale now though it is not safe to plant them out of doors except in the mildest parts of the country. Even if the plants are not actually killed by frost, they may receive such a severe check from cold May nights that they never completely recover to give a proper display. It is far better to delay bedding out until at least the last week in May.

Stake the flower spikes of herbaceous plants as they develop, and pay particular attention to delphiniums and lupins. Where the shoots of delphiniums are over-crowded they should be thinned out.

Growers of exhibition sweet peas will be kept busy from now on removing the sideshoots and tying in the main stems. Sweet peas can be fed but do not use fertiliser with a high nitrogen content as this may aggravate bud dropping. In the North, it is about the right time to plant sweet peas.

Plant outdoor-flowering chrysanthemums in the ground already prepared. Be sure to plant firmly and make certain that the soil ball rests on the bottom of the hole.

FRUIT

The tying in of the young growth of wall-trained peaches and nectarines should begin. Loop the young shoots to the branch from which they are growing to encourage them to grow in the right direction.

Watch gooseberry bushes closely for any sign of aphids or caterpillars and spray with derris if necessary.

Newly planted fruit trees appreciate an early evening spraying with clear water to speed up their development.

VEGETABLES

The earliest Brussels sprout plants may now be planted out and it is these first plants which usually produce the best sprouts. There is frequently a tendency among amateur gardeners to plant them too closely, and if they are planted 3 ft. apart each way the result will be far better sprouts and a heavier crop. The space need not be wasted as early-hearting cabbage or early cauliflowers can be planted between the sprouts and will be off the ground before the sprouts need more space.

If club root has been troublesome, dip the roots of the Brussels sprouts, cabbages and cauliflowers in a paste made with water and 4 per cent. calomel dust before planting.

Sow more peas for succession and between the pea rows sow more lettuce or spinach – another way of using the ground most economically.

Again, it is important not to stint on space for peas. Leave plenty of room between the rows so that the plants get the benefit of full light. Peas which grow 3 ft. tall should be given at least 3 ft. of space between the rows.

Sow seeds of heading broccoli (autumn-, winter- and spring-heading) and kale.

Seed of sweet corn can be sown out of doors now where the plants are to mature.

GREENHOUSE
Bedding plants must be properly hardened off ready for

Planting brassica seedlings with a dibber. Note the line which is used to ensure that plants are inserted in straight rows

May: week 1

planting out at the end of the month or in early June.

Topdress tuberous begonias which were potted a few weeks ago with a little John Innes No. 2 Potting Compost.

Attend to watering regularly. It is surprising how quickly pot plants can dry out when the weather is really bright. Give sufficient water to soak right through the pot.

Specimen pelargonium (geranium) plants for winter flowering should be potted this month. Use the John Innes No. 2 Potting Compost.

When the first flower buds can be seen in the tip of each tomato plant they will be ready to plant out in the border or for moving on into 9-in. pots or large boxes – or rings if the ring-culture method is to be adopted. John Innes No. 3 Potting Compost should be used in the containers for this move, and if planting in the border make sure that it consists of a good loamy mixture. I like to dig well-rotted manure or peat into the soil and give a sprinkling of bonemeal as well as a dressing of 2 oz. of organic-based fertiliser per square yard. When the first truss of fruit has set, feed the plants once a week.

Celery and celeriac seedlings should be pricked out.

Staking the flower spikes of a delphinium. If possible it is best to put one cane to each spike to give maximum support

FLOWERS

In sheltered gardens and on light, well-drained soils half-hardy annuals can be sown out of doors in the next week or so. Those to sow include ageratums, nemesias, *Mesembryanthemum criniflorum*, French and African marigolds and zinnias. Look over hardy annuals which were sown earlier and thin them out if necessary.

As soon as *Prunus triloba* has finished flowering cut back the shoots that have flowered to encourage strong new growths for next year's flowers. Flowering currants, too, can be pruned as soon as flowering has finished by cutting out some of the older wood and removing any weak growth.

Stop outdoor-flowering chrysanthemums by pinching out the young centre tip of each plant.

As rambler roses begin to make strong shoots from the base, these should be carefully tied in, for if they are left unsupported they are liable to be damaged.

If the weather is dry keep a careful watch on newly planted trees and shrubs. It is a very good plan to spray them over in the evenings during dry spells. Then, after a heavy shower of rain, mulch around them with several inches of well-rotted manure or compost to conserve moisture.

FRUIT

Greenfly (aphids) can cause serious blistering of black currant foliage, and spraying should be carried out against these pests before the leaves have curled. Derris or malathion can be used and, as always when using sprays, the manufacturer's instructions should be followed strictly. Morello and dessert cherries should also be sprayed against blackfly and if apple trees were not sprayed earlier, this, too, can be done now.

Put clean straw around strawberries to protect the fruit from mud splashing, making sure that it is tucked well under the plants. Alternatives are straw mats or black polythene.

May: week 2

Apricots will need thinning, especially where small fruits are clustered very closely together. A few should be removed but this job should not be completed until the stones have formed (see p. 79).

If peach leaf curl disease begins to show on peaches and nectarines, pick off affected leaves immediately and burn them.

Plant out melons from their 3-in. pots. These can be grown in frames, under cloches or in the greenhouse.

VEGETABLES

Use a hoe to keep onion rows clear of weeds and thin the plants where necessary. After hoeing dust along the rows with BHC to keep onion fly away.

Both runner and French beans can be sown with safety out of doors now. Prior to sowing, dust the soil with a general fertiliser at the rate of 2 oz. to the square yard.

With runner beans, I like to sow one seed at each string or cane and put in a few surplus ones at the end of the row to fill any gaps. The seeds are sown in a double row, allowing a space of 12 in. between the rows and 9 to 12 in. between the seeds in the rows. Cover them with 2 in. of soil.

Tucking clean straw under the leaves of strawberry plants to prevent the fruits from being splashed by rain and mud

Sow French beans in drills 1 in. deep and space them 9 in. apart in a double row with 6 in. between the rows.

Thin beetroot seedlings to 9 in. apart as soon as the leaves touch. Do this with all successive sowings.

Thin carrots to 9 in. apart. Continue to make sowings to provide continuity, thinning as necessary.

The ground can now be prepared for the planting of outdoor tomatoes later this month. The best position for them is against a south-facing wall or fence. Tomatoes like a good, rich soil containing plenty of rotted manure.

GREENHOUSE

In many districts it should be safe to stand bedding plants outside, in the shelter of a wall, to harden them off.

It will be necessary to shade the greenhouse now for begonias, gloxinias and many other plants need some protection from the sun. The most inexpensive way of doing this is to coat the glass with whitewash or one of the proprietary shading compounds.

Stake and tie perpetual-flowering carnations, or use the split rings especially designed for this purpose. Many plants will be ready for their final move into 8-in. pots using the John Innes No. 1 Potting Compost.

Tuberous-rooted begonias can be fed as the plants fill their pots with roots. Once they begin to show flower buds, feed them once a week with liquid fertiliser.

This is the latest time to take hydrangea cuttings to produce good flowering plants for next year. Choose strong non-flowering shoots, 4 to 5 in. long, and trim cleanly just below a joint. Root them round the edge of $3\frac{1}{2}$-in. pots in a mixture of equal parts peat and sand, these being placed in a propagating frame with a temperature of 16°C. (60°F.).

Make a sowing of *Primula malacoides* to provide plants for flowering during the winter.

Coleus plants raised from seed should now be potted on into 5-in. pots. Use the John Innes No. 1 Potting Compost.

May: week 3

FLOWERS

Many of the bulbous plants will have finished flowering by now, and quite apart from the desirability of keeping the garden tidy, it is wise to pinch off the dead flower heads to prevent seeds forming. The foliage, however, must be left to die down naturally for the stems and leaves help to build up the bulbs and so ensure that they flower well next year.

Watch for signs of aphids on roses. They can do a lot of damage to young shoots, particularly after continual cold winds, when roses and other plants are not able to grow freely. A spray can be used containing BHC insecticide, and it is worth while to add a fungicide, such as captan, to control black spot at the same time.

Grass, and weeds growing in the grass on lawns, will be growing freely at this time of year, and it is an ideal time to use a selective weedkiller. This will control most troublesome lawn weeds, but every care should be taken to prevent the chemical from blowing on to the plants and shrubs near the lawn. Treatment should only be carried out on a very still day.

Many lawn fertilisers now contain selective weedkillers, and if these are used, feeding and weeding can be done in one operation.

Two weeds which have become troublesome in lawns over recent years are the blue-flowered speedwell and yellow suckling clover. Most selective weedkillers have little effect on these but there is now a weedkiller based on morfamquat which will eradicate even these difficult weeds.

Polyanthus seedlings raised from a sowing made in the greenhouse in March can now be pricked out into a nursery bed. If they are rather small it is wise to shade them with a few leafy branches and spray them with water when the weather is hot.

Seeds of wallflowers, Sweet Williams, Canterbury Bells and other biennials should be sown in the North now, a couple of weeks earlier than in the South. This gives the plants the longer growing season they require in such climatic conditions.

FRUIT

Apple trees sometimes grow very strongly and produce few flowers. This means that crops will be poor and one way to curb the growth is to bark ring the trees. If the whole tree is growing too vigorously the ring of bark can be taken out from around the main stem, but if one branch has a tendency to grow strongly it is only necessary to ring the branch concerned. The ring must be no more than $\frac{1}{2}$ in. wide, and should go down as far as the wood. Afterwards, seal the cut with adhesive tape.

Wall-trained fruit trees may need watering as the soil at the base of walls tends to dry out quickly.

VEGETABLES

The latest Brussels sprouts should be planted now. They need a really long season in which to grow to maturity so it is important that they should be planted out as early as possible. Give them ample space – at least 3 ft. apart each

Applying selective weedkiller with the aid of a dribble bar attachment on a watering-can

May: week 3

way. It is worth noting that the newer F_1 hybrids are more compact plants than other kinds and so need less space. They produce very good, solid sprouts, too, which are uniformly sized.

Prepare cold frames for planting cucumbers. I find it best to put a mound of soil, in which some rotted manure or peat has been incorporated, in the centre of each frame and to plant one cucumber in the centre of each mound.

GREENHOUSE

A hanging basket of pelargoniums, fuchsias, ferns or pendulous begonias adds beauty and interest to a greenhouse or conservatory. They do, however, need regular watering and more baskets are spoilt by under- than by over-watering. From now on feed the baskets at least once a week.

Seeds of cinerarias and large-flowered calceolarias may be sown now in pots and placed in a cold frame. Cinerarias can be sown at intervals between April and late June to give a succession of plants, the first of which will flower at the turn of the year. Calceolarias are sown between May and July and these will flower from April until early June of the following year.

Old cyclamen corms will now have finished their growth and water should be gradually reduced so that the corms can be given a short rest. Do not, however, allow them to dry off completely.

Tuberous begonias and gloxinias raised from seed sown in February will need potting up into 3- or $3\frac{1}{2}$-in. pots filled with John Innes No. 1 Potting Compost. Warm, humid and shady surroundings are needed for successful growth.

Seedlings of *Primula obconica* and *P. sinensis* should be pricked out before they become overcrowded in the seed boxes. Use John Innes No. 1 Potting Compost.

May: week 4

FLOWERS

Now is the time to plant summer bedding plants. Wallflowers and other spring-flowering plants may still look attractive and it is tempting to leave them a little longer, but as soon as the flowers begin to fade the plants should be pulled out to make way for the summer bedding subjects. The beds must be dug over and some peat or garden compost dug in to help to retain moisture.

The lovely early-flowering *Clematis montana* and its pink-flowered form, *rubens,* can be pruned as soon as flowering has finished.

It is a good idea to put a small stick against the best polyanthus so that after flowering has finished they may be lifted and divided. This splitting up is usually done in about the middle of June, but, of course, the plants must be marked when they are at their best. As I lift the plants I divide them into separate crowns, pulling them apart with roots attached to each crown. To make sure that they are free from aphids and red spider, each one is dipped into a good insecticide before planting. It is best to plant in positions where the soil is fairly moist and there is partial shade.

As auriculas finish flowering, they can be lifted and divided for planting out in a similar manner to polyanthus. This is also a good time for lifting and dividing *Primula* Wanda, *P. rosea* and *P. denticulata.*

Persistent weeds such as bindweed and ground elder growing between shrubs and other plants can be spot treated with selective weedkiller. This may be brushed on to the weeds or applied with a small sprayer, though I would emphasise the importance of choosing a still day.

It is now time to prepare for planting rooted dahlia cuttings. Dahlias like a good well-worked soil to which rotted manure, compost or moist peat has been added, as well as a dressing of a general, organic-based fertiliser applied at the rate of 2 oz. to the square yard. The stakes

May: week 4

for the dahlias can also be put in place, ready for planting
in early June.

Sow seed outside of *Alyssum saxatile* and aubrieta.

FRUIT

Raspberries are producing an abundance of young shoots
from the base of the plants, and if these are thinned now
the new canes required for next year's fruiting will be
stronger and better. Sucker growths which appear well
out of the rows can be cut off with a hoe.

Spray apple trees at petal fall as a further protection
against scab. Use lime sulphur or captan, and add BHC to
kill maggots which damage the fruits.

Continue to tie in young growths on peaches and nectarines as they develop, and pinch out the young side
growths on wall-trained plums when they have made
about six leaves. Where growths are needed to fill a bare
space on the wall these should be trained into position
without pinching.

Netting used to cover strawberries should be examined
and any holes repaired. The sooner these nets are in position the better.

VEGETABLES

It should now be safe to plant out runner beans which
have been raised in pots or boxes. Where French beans
are growing under cloches keep them well supplied with
water. This applies to other vegetables under cloches.

More peas can be sown for succession. Sticks can be
placed in position for peas from sowings made earlier.

Cucumbers can now be planted in cold frames but do
not plant too deeply. If the base of the stem is buried,
water is likely to collect and cause rotting of the stem,
known as foot rot.

Potatoes should be earthed up regularly, and if the
ground is hard, lightly fork over the soil in the rows to
make earthing up easier. A little fertiliser sprinkled between the rows before earthing up will also help.

Prepare the ground for planting out frame-raised vegetable marrow plants. The actual planting should be done next week. Dig a hole 2 ft. wide and $1\frac{1}{2}$ ft. deep, put a 9-in. layer of well-rotted manure or garden compost in the bottom and return the soil.

GREENHOUSE

Verbenas in pots need regular staking and tying, and a weekly feed throughout the summer to keep them healthy.

Pelargonium (geranium) cuttings may be taken now and these will make good plants for winter flowering.

Any shrubs grown in pots should be plunged outside by now. Keep them well watered throughout the summer.

Plants of *Begonia semperflorens* can be bedded out now or next week. Alternatively, they can be grown as pot plants in 6-in. pots. They are excellent for display in the sun lounge or conservatory.

Planting out summer bedding plants. These will soon grow and give an attractive display of flowers

June: week 1

FLOWERS

The weather should be getting warmer now and possibly drier, so remember that bedding plants put out last month may need watering. They have not yet anchored themselves to the soil and if allowed to become dry they could soon deteriorate.

Although the grass where daffodils have been flowering may look untidy it must not be cut until the foliage has died down. If the bulbs have been growing there for several years and are not flowering well, they are probably overcrowded and could do with lifting and dividing.

Herbaceous plants and lilies should be staked carefully as the stems develop to prevent wind damage.

This is a good time to sow seeds of *Primula denticulata, P. rosea* and *P. Wanda* for it should be ripe now.

Greenfly can be very troublesome and regular spraying is necessary, particularly on roses, to prevent damage.

In the Midlands and South, wallflowers, forget-me-nots, Canterbury Bells, Sweet Williams, foxgloves and many other biennials can be raised from seed sown now. Remember to water them if the weather turns dry.

Take care never to allow sweet pea plants to become dry, and feed them regularly with a general fertiliser.

Moving a chrysanthemum into its final pot. 1. The plant is held steady with one hand, while compost is added with the other. 2. To help firm the new compost, a wooden rammer can be used. 3. Staking is very important as the plant develops, and three large canes are inserted for later use

FRUIT

The small white maggots so often found in raspberries are the grubs of the raspberry beetle and they can be controlled by spraying with derris. Where this pest has been troublesome in the past, give a second spraying about 10 days after the first application.

Suckers which sprout up from the base of plum, damson and other fruit trees should be dug out.

As soon as gooseberries are large enough for bottling or cooking some of them can be picked. The rest of the berries should remain on the bushes to attain their full size, but they must be protected with netting otherwise they will be damaged by birds. Mildew is often troublesome with this crop, attacking the tips of the shoots. If infection is seen, in spite of an earlier spraying with lime sulphur (see p. 52), the affected shoots should be nipped out and burnt and the bushes sprayed again with a solution of dinocap.

Blackfly can be a nuisance on dessert cherries and it is wise to spray regularly with malathion to prevent damage to the young shoots and leaves. Alternatively, use a systemic insecticide which will be effective for a much longer period. Remember that the manufacturer's instructions must always be followed when using chemicals in the garden.

June: week 1

VEGETABLES

Marrows and courgettes can be planted out in positions already prepared. Sweet corn can also be planted if seeds were sown in 3-in. pots towards the end of April.

Plant celery in prepared trenches (see p. 40), spacing the plants 10 to 12 in. apart. Water well after planting.

Celeriac, too, can be planted now. The soil does not need to be so rich for this crop as for celery and planting is not done in trenches. Space the plants 1 ft. apart with $1\frac{1}{2}$ ft. between the rows. No earthing up is necessary.

A sowing of white turnips can be made between pea rows or along the sides of runner bean rows.

It should now be safe to plant tomatoes out of doors.

GREENHOUSE

The final potting of chrysanthemums must be completed. Afterwards, stand the plants outside in rows on an ash base. Pot the plants on into 8-in. pots using the John Innes No. 3 Potting Compost and leave a space at the top for topdressing later. Support the plants with canes tied to wires stretched between posts at a height of 4 ft.

Cyclamen should now be potted on into their final 6-in. pots using the John Innes No. 2 Potting Compost with a little extra coarse sand added. These plants need cool, moist, shady conditions in the summer and a cold frame is ideal.

Hydrangea cuttings should be potted individually in 3-in. pots as soon as they are well rooted.

Arum lilies may now be stood out of doors to give them a rest; or, better still, the pots can be laid on their sides under a west- or south-facing wall.

Pot solanums up into their final 5- or 6-in. pots, using John Innes No. 1 Potting Compost.

Begin watering poinsettias which have been resting. This will encourage the production of new growths from which cuttings can be made by the end of the month.

FLOWERS

A job which I like to see done regularly is the edging of grass verges. If this can be done at frequent intervals, the trimmings need not be swept up.

As alpine plants in the rock garden finish flowering trim them back to keep the plants compact and to encourage them to make good growth for flowering next spring. Any gaps in the rock garden can be filled with bedding plants.

Flea beetle can damage wallflower seedlings badly so dust along the rows frequently with derris powder or BHC.

Canes should now be put in position for gladioli so that the flower spikes can be tied to them with soft string as they develop.

As tulips finish flowering, lift the bulbs and, if they are still growing strongly, heel them in elsewhere. Otherwise, dry them off and store until replanting time.

FRUIT

The young shoots of blackberries and loganberries are very brittle, so as they grow keep them tied to the supporting wires.

I like to see cordon gooseberries trained against the wall of a house. This is a good way of growing this fruit when space is limited and where dessert fruits of good size are desired. Keep young side growths pinched back regularly, and give an occasional spray with derris to prevent caterpillars eating the foliage.

Continue the training of peaches and nectarines by tying in the young shoots regularly. As the fruits form, feed the trees with a general fertiliser (applied at the rate of 4 oz. per tree) and afterwards water the fertiliser into the ground. A thick mulch of garden compost or manure to follow will also help. The fruits must be thinned to about 9 in. apart. This can be done now or it can be left until after the stones have formed.

June: week 2

VEGETABLES

Cucumbers in frames must be stopped regularly by pinching out the growing tips. Four laterals will develop, and these are trained to the corners of the frame. They should be stopped at the fourth leaf. Topdress with fresh compost before the soil is completely covered.

Early broad beans will have set about three clusters of flowers and can be stopped by pinching out the growing tip. This will encourage pods to form and help prevent blackfly damage as this pest likes young shoots.

Spinach seedlings raised from a sowing made in May should be thinned to 9 in. apart.

Early potatoes should be lifted and the site prepared for planting leeks.

To keep onions growing sturdily, water when the soil is dry and give a weekly feed of a general fertiliser, applied at the rate of 1 oz. to each yard of row.

Shallots, too, will benefit from the application of a general fertiliser, applied in this case at the rate of 2 oz. to each yard of row. Note, however, that this is a single dressing, unlike that recommended for onions.

GREENHOUSE

Cineraria and large-flowered calceolaria seedlings should be pricked out as soon as possible into boxes filled with John Innes No. 1 Potting Compost. Give them a light position with shade from strong sunshine.

Cyclamen should be moved into cold frames. The lights must be shaded as these plants do not like strong sun. Spray the plants over each morning and evening, and after the later spray, close the lights to conserve heat.

The yellow-flowered *Genista fragrans* can be propagated from cuttings taken now. These should be rooted in a warm propagating frame. Plants which have finished flowering can be trimmed back and repotted.

Grape thinning is a task requiring frequent attention at this time of year. Surplus berries should be removed with

long, pointed scissors. Start at the bottom of the bunch
and work gradually upwards, removing small, seedless
berries first. Use a small forked stick to isolate berries
which are to be removed as in this way it is possible to
avoid touching the berries which remain and perhaps
spoiling their bloom.

Mid-season chrysanthemums, such as Loveliness, can
be stopped for the second time.

Tuberous begonias need careful staking and it may be
necessary to support the large flowers. Feed the plants
each week to keep them growing sturdily.

Achimenes also need supporting and I find that twiggy
sticks are best. Insert them around the edge of the pots.

As the flowers fade on established hydrangeas, cut
back the stems and repot the plants. Afterwards, they can
be stood out of doors for the summer.

Spray chrysanthemums with an insecticide at regular
intervals to keep down aphids, capsid bugs and leaf
miner. A compatible fungicide could be incorporated
with the insecticide to give protection against mildew.

Pot on coleus plants raised from cuttings into their
final 5-in. pots, using John Innes No. 1 Potting Compost.

*If tulips are still growing
strongly when the time comes
for lifting, they should be
heeled in elsewhere until
growth has finished*

June: week 3

FLOWERS

At times when the weather is dry for long periods, watering is one of the most important tasks in the garden. Give the plants a good soaking for if the surface soil only is moistened it will encourage the plants to make surface roots which are more likely to suffer from drought. Shrubs and other plants growing under trees often suffer from a shortage of water, so give these particular attention.

Always cut the seed pods from lupins and delphiniums as soon as the flowers fade for this encourages them to give a second display in July or August.

If you want especially good rose blooms, the clusters of buds should be reduced to one each. It is best to retain the centre bud as this will be most advanced. Disbudding should be carried out at an early stage of development, and is usually only done to hybrid teas.

If last winter was severe and hydrangeas had their flower buds killed, cut back the stems which would have carried flowers so that any buds emerging from near the base will have the benefit of extra light. Any thin or poor shoots are best removed altogether.

Aubrieta and *Alyssum saxatile* seedlings raised from sowings made earlier can now be pricked out in a nursery bed. Afterwards, shade the young plants from strong sunshine for a few days.

Low-growing bedding plants such as verbenas and ivy-leaved geraniums can be pegged down so that they cover the soil with a continuous carpet of growth and flowers. Use pieces of galvanised wire bent like hairpins.

A place should be found in every garden for winter-flowering pansies. Sow the seed in boxes and put these in a cold frame. When the resulting seedlings are large enough, prick them out into boxes of John Innes No. 1 Potting Compost. When well established they can be planted out.

FRUIT

Vines growing out of doors can be stopped now. New side growths should have their growing points pinched out at two leaves beyond the embryo bunches of fruit. Secondary growths should be stopped after the first leaf, and tendrils should also be pinched out. Do not allow any side growths to carry more than one bunch of fruit.

Apricot fruits should be thinned now, if the stones have formed. It is not always essential to do this, especially if the flowers failed to set well. Apples and pears can also be given an initial thinning. This task must not be carried out drastically though, as there may well be some fruits which will fall naturally.

In the North spray or dust raspberries with derris as a protection against raspberry beetle.

As dessert cherries begin to ripen, protect them from birds, or there will be little fruit left to harvest.

VEGETABLES

Leeks can be planted now, and for general purposes the best way is to make planting holes 6 to 8 in. deep with a large dibber. One leek can be dropped into each plant-

Removing the seed pods from a lupin. If this is done promptly, a second display of flowers will appear in July or August

June: week 3

ing hole which is then well watered. Sufficient soil should be carried into the hole with the water to cover the roots and no more filling in is necessary.

Savoy and January King cabbages can also be planted.

More peas can be sown for succession, but the drills must be well watered before sowing. While on the subject of watering, if the weather is dry drench all vegetables, especially peas, runner beans and celery.

Sow more lettuce seeds now. I would also suggest having a row of parsley for winter and spring use.

GREENHOUSE
Tomatoes should be ripening fast now, and the fruit must be picked regularly. If some of the fruits are showing signs of greenback, water the plants with a solution of 1 oz. of sulphate of potash in a gallon of water.

One of the most valuable winter- and spring-flowering plants for the amateur gardener is *Primula malacoides*. Sow the seed in pots or boxes of seed compost and germinate in a temperature of 13 to 16°C. (55 to 60°F.).

Young hydrangeas raised from cuttings will probably be in need of stopping. In any case, this task must not be done later than mid-July, otherwise the side growths would be made too late to flower well the next spring.

Perpetual-flowering carnations should be potted on into 8-in. pots using John Innes No. 1 Potting Compost if this has not already been done.

It is at this time of year that carnations can be spoilt by aphids, thrips and red spider mites. Use a BHC fumigant or a malathion spray against aphids. Fumigate with azobenzene against red spider mite, or spray with water, for this pest thrives in dry conditions. Fumigate or spray with BHC against thrips.

Pot winter-flowering begonias on into 4- or 5-in. pots using the John Innes No. 2 Potting Compost.

FLOWERS

Roses are now at their best, and it does no harm if the flowers are cut regularly. When cutting, make sure that sharp secateurs are used, and cut immediately above a strong bud at a leaf joint. This will encourage the bud into early growth, which will mean more flowers later on. Suckers which appear from below ground level should be cut away as near to the rootstock as possible.

The tall bearded irises have now finished flowering, and where the rhizomes are crowded they should be lifted and divided. Select firm young pieces of rhizome and discard the old parts from the centre. Cut back the leaves to about 9 in. Irises like a rich soil and a sunny, open position. With planting completed, the top of the rhizome should show just above the soil.

Take cuttings of alpines such as dianthus to fill bare spaces in the rock garden. Root them in a sandy compost in a cold frame and plant out in the autumn.

If lawns are fed now with lawn fertiliser they should keep a good colour for the rest of the summer and autumn.

Gardens with large trees are often troubled with capsid bugs which can do a lot of damage to fuchsias, dahlias and chrysanthemums. They can also spoil the late-summer blooms of the pretty blue-flowered shrub caryopteris, so I like to spray every 10 to 14 days with BHC. Rock roses and sun roses can also be badly damaged so spray these as well.

I have mentioned chrysanthemums in connection with capsid bugs. Watch out also for leaf miner, aphids and earwigs on this plant. All can be kept down with BHC.

Prune weigelas, philadelphuses, deutzias and escallonias as soon as their flowers fade to encourage new growth.

FRUIT

Raspberry picking is in full swing, and as the fruits ripen quickly in warm weather the canes should be looked over every two or three days. If you do not possess a fruit cage, protect the canes against birds with netting. Keep the plants mulched with straw or strawy manure.

Strawberry plants which have been earmarked for the production of runners should have these thinned to no more than six strong runners to each plant.

Melons must be stopped by pinching out the tips of the shoots one or two leaves beyond the young melons. Secondary growth should be stopped beyond the second leaf.

VEGETABLES

Carrots and beetroot raised from sowings made in late May and early June will now be ready for thinning.

Cucumbers growing in frames must be stopped regularly. As young cucumbers begin to form, place a slate underneath to keep them off the soil.

To help rhubarb plants to build up good crowns for next year, flower spikes should be removed and the plants well watered and fed.

To protect the curds of early cauliflowers, turn the inner leaves over them. As cauliflowers and summer cabbages are cut, the stems and roots should be pulled up and burnt to prevent the spread of club root and cabbage root fly.

In dry weather thrips can play havoc with peas. At the first sign of attack spray with malathion or BHC.

Runner and French beans are likely to be badly affected by blackfly and it is best to spray with a systemic insecticide to keep the plants free of these pests.

GREENHOUSE

When the weather is hot, plants which have filled their pots with roots may need watering twice a day.

Plants of *Azalea indica* should be plunged outside from the end of June to September. Choose a site in partial shade and bury the pots up to their rims. Continue to feed at 14-day intervals throughout the summer.

Late-flowering chrysanthemums must be stopped for the last time now. Overhead spraying will be helpful.

Solanum capsicastrum, the Winter Cherry, does not always set its fruits freely, but daily spraying with water will help. The plants should be out of doors now and should be fed once a week with liquid fertiliser until November, and watered freely.

Freesias which were raised from seed sown earlier can now be stood out of doors in a sheltered place, or they can be grown in a cold frame during the summer.

Tuberous begonias and gloxinias grown from seed should be ready for potting into their final 5- or 6-in. pots. Use the John Innes No. 2 Potting Compost. These plants will be in flower from late July until October.

Tuberous begonias raised from tubers can be potted on into 7-in. pots if really large specimens are wanted.

Sow cyclamen seed in boxes or pots of seed compost, and provide them with a temperature of 16°C. (60°F.)

White flies can be a nuisance in the greenhouse as they reproduce so rapidly. They are particularly troublesome where tomatoes are being grown and it is wise to fumigate the house at 10- to 14-day intervals with BHC smoke pellets or cones.

Bending the inner leaves of a cauliflower over the curd to protect it from sun and rain and keep it clean and white

July: week 1

FLOWERS

As roses approach the end of their first flush of flowering, feed them with a rose or general organic fertiliser to help the second batch of flowers.

Outdoor chrysanthemums will also be in need of feeding, and it is a fertiliser fairly rich in potash which is needed.

Privet hedges must be clipped fairly frequently if they are to be kept neat and tidy, and this is even more important in the case of young hedges to ensure that the plants make dense, well-branched growth.

Garden pinks of all kinds can be increased by cuttings or pipings taken now. The only difference between cuttings and pipings is that the former are severed with a knife or razor blade just beneath a joint, whereas pipings are carefully pulled out at a joint.

From now onwards, dead flowers should be removed regularly from plants as one walks around the garden for this encourages them to go on flowering and, of course, it keeps the garden neat and tidy.

If the weather is dry, I water my standard fuchsias at least once a week. I also feed them regularly with a compound fertiliser.

Hardy primulas such as *Primula japonica* and *P. pulverulenta* can be lifted and divided after flowering.

Greenhouse chrysanthemums, which are now standing outside for the summer, should be fed regularly to encourage growth

FRUIT

Strawberry runners on plants selected for propagation can be pegged into pots filled with potting soil and sunk into the ground around the parent plants. Keep the layers watered, and when they have rooted well, sever them from the parent plants.

Strawberry beds which are three years or more old have outlived their usefulness and should be discarded.

VEGETABLES

Some of the earlier crops such as potatoes, early peas and broad beans have finished and should be cleared away as quickly as possible to make room for various catchcrops such as shorthorn carrots and globe beetroot. It is also worth making a further sowing of a dwarf, early-maturing pea such as Meteor or Kelvedon Wonder.

A late savoy cabbage such as Ormskirk can be sown now where the plants can be left to mature. Sow the seed thinly and then reduce the seedlings to 15 or 18 in. apart. The winter cabbage, January King, should be planted now without delay, and this is also the latest time for planting out autumn-heading cauliflower and broccoli. Plant broccoli $2\frac{1}{2}$ ft. apart for it needs plenty of room for expansion as the plants are big and leafy. All brassicas like firm ground.

Celery must be watered freely whenever the weather is dry, for it is a moisture-loving plant. If it is allowed to become dry it is likely to run to seed. Dusting with BHC will help to keep off the celery fly.

Potatoes should be sprayed now with Bordeaux mixture as a precaution against potato blight.

GREENHOUSE

This is the latest time for cutting back established hydrangeas after flowering. If this were done later the plants would not have sufficient time to make new growth for next year's flowering.

July: week 1

Young hydrangea plants should be moved into 5-in. pots. Use the John Innes No. 2 Potting Compost. By mid-July they should have their growing tips removed so that they make bushy plants. After stopping, move the plants to a cold frame. Remember to keep them well watered.

Chrysanthemums, which should be standing outdoors now in their pots, will need regular tying, in addition to watering and feeding. Make sure that the stakes are strong enough to do their job properly.

Tuberous begonias should be disbudded. It is the small side buds of the female flowers that must be removed. Remember that these plants do not like an over-dry atmosphere as this will cause bud dropping.

Young plants of perpetual-flowering carnations are now better in a frame than in the greenhouse. Give the plants their final stopping to encourage a succession of flowers later on. The sideshoots should be stopped at four pairs of leaves. When the pots are full of roots feed them once a week with a high potash fertiliser.

This is the ideal time to propagate *Begonia rex* from leaf cuttings. Slit the veins on well-developed leaves and lay these, with the stem in the soil, on a mixture of sand and peat. Small stones placed on the leaves will keep the veins in contact with the rooting medium. Place the leaf cuttings in a temperature of 16 to 18°C. (60 to 65°F.) and shade them if necessary. The young plants which develop should be potted individually using John Innes No. 1 Potting Compost.

The Rex begonias are grown mainly for their very handsome leaves, and one of the best known is the showy *B. masoniana* whose leaves are marked with a prominent pattern like an Iron Cross. These begonias should never be dried off and they need a minimum winter temperature of 10°C. (50°F.) and shade from strong sunshine in summer.

FLOWERS

The many flower shows held up and down the country each summer provide a splendid opportunity to see the new roses. It is a good idea to make a note of these straightaway so that you can order them while stocks are still available.

It is wise to spray all roses now against greenfly and mildew. I find that a combined insecticide and fungicide containing BHC and dinocap controls most troubles.

This is the time of year when I layer border carnations and pinks (dianthus). Only good, healthy plants should be selected, and sturdy, non-flowering shoots are the ones which are actually layered. Replace some of the soil around each plant to be layered with potting compost so that the layers have a good rooting medium.

Cuttings can be taken between now and the end of August from *Begonia semperflorens* used in bedding displays. Root them in the greenhouse in a temperature of 18°C. (65°F.). They will flower as pot plants during the winter.

Outdoor chrysanthemums need good support as their stems are brittle and easily broken by wind and rain. If the stakes were not put in at planting time, this should be done immediately. Take care to make them firm.

The feeding of dahlias should begin now, but be careful to keep the fertiliser away from the stems. A mulch of lawn mowings or garden compost will help a lot as dahlias like moisture. The taller varieties must be securely staked as heavy shoots are easily snapped off.

FRUIT

Strawberry runners in pots should be watered regularly.

Pears, plums and even dessert cherries will all repay careful thinning if there has been a heavy set of fruit.

Now is the time, also, to complete the thinning of outdoor grapes and to spray the vines with dispersible sulphur or Bordeaux mixture against mildew and other fungi.

July: week 2

Melons grown under cloches or in frames and greenhouses are ready for pollinating. It is essential to hand pollinate the flowers and not to leave it to nature. The female flowers can be recognised by the small embryo fruit behind the flower. All the female flowers on a plant should be fertilised at the same time with pollen from the male flowers. At this time, also, all shoots should be pinched out at one or two leaves beyond the point at which the fruit is forming.

VEGETABLES
Continue to sprinkle fertiliser between the onion rows. Apply at the rate of 1 oz. to a yard of row and hoe it in carefully.

If flowers appear on shallots these should be removed.

Spinach beet and seakale beet (Swiss chard) are two vegetables not sufficiently grown in gardens. These are profitable crops which give a supply of edible leaves over a long period. Seeds of both these vegetables can be sown now.

Mulch along the sides of the rows of runner beans with lawn mowings, garden compost or even straw. The object is not so much to feed the beans as to retain the moisture in the soil. But do not forget to water the soil thoroughly before applying the mulch, and pull the mulch back at intervals to make sure that the soil is still moist.

Cucumbers in frames will need regular watering and feeding, and the laterals should be stopped at intervals.

More round-seeded spinach can be sown for continuity. Make the sowings in drills 1 in. deep and 1 ft. apart in ground which has been well dug and well manured. Thin the seedlings to 9 in. apart.

More lettuce and salad onions can also be sown.

GREENHOUSE
Grapes growing in unheated greenhouses will now probably be in need of their final thinning. Pay particular

attention to the shoulders of each bunch where over-crowding is likely to occur. Use the narrow, pointed scissors needed for this job with great care.

Regal pelargoniums should be moved outside for the next few weeks. Cuttings may be taken from these plants now. Make them from firm, young, non-flowering growths, 3 to 5 in. in length. Trim cleanly just below a leaf, remove the lower leaves and dip in hormone rooting powder before placing round the edge of 3½-in. pots filled with a mixture of 1 part loam, 2 parts peat and 3 parts coarse sand. If extra sand is spread over the compost, some will trickle down into the bottom of each hole as the cuttings are inserted and will assist rooting. After watering in, place the pots on the greenhouse bench and, if shaded from direct sunshine and syringed once or twice a day, they should root without trouble.

Cinerarias should be potted singly before they become overcrowded. Put them into 3½-in. pots of John Innes No. 1 Potting Compost and keep them in a cool place, such as a cold frame, during the summer.

Pick off the flower buds of coleus plants and pinch out the growing tip of each plant to encourage bushy growth and the production of more colourful leaves.

Spray cyclamen with clear water in the morning and evening in warm weather.

Hand pollinating the female flowers of a melon with a male flower that has been stripped of its petals

July: week 3

FLOWERS

If the season has been kind, seedling wallflowers, Sweet Williams, Canterbury Bells and other biennials should be ready for transplanting into a nursery bed, 9 in. apart in rows 9 to 12 in. apart. They need good soil and an open situation.

Dahlias will almost certainly need some thinning, particularly where old tubers have been planted rather than rooted cuttings.

This is the time to bud roses. *Rosa canina, R. laxa* and *R. rugosa* are the stocks most frequently used. The latter is easy to work and is often used for standards. It is, however, prone to suckering.

Suitable buds come from half-ripened rose shoots of the current season's growth. The aim is to have a small, shield-shaped portion of green rind with a dormant bud and a leaf stalk by which it can be held. The thin sliver of wood at the back of the shield should be removed by lifting it carefully with a knife. The bud is now inserted in the T-shaped incision made in the bark of the stock and firmly tied with raffia. Bush roses are budded just below ground level on the main stem. Standards are budded on the main stem at the desired height of the head.

Wait three or four weeks before inspecting the buds. If they are fresh and plump they have probably taken. Con-

Budding a rose bush. 1. A bud is prepared by cutting a shield-shaped portion of the rind and including with it a leaf stalk and a dormant bud in its axil. 2. The prepared bud is inserted in a T-shaped incision on the main stem of the rootstock. 3. The bud is then firmly tied in position with raffia

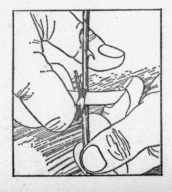

versely, dry, shrivelled buds have failed and must be re-worked.

FRUIT

Now is the time to give apples their final thinning. If the king fruit has not already been removed, this is the one which should go. The king fruit is in the centre of each cluster, and it is seldom of such good shape as the others.

Gooseberries should be sprayed to keep down caterpillars, greenfly and other pests, but it is very important to make sure that the spray used is a safe one, as harvesting will be in a week or two from now. Derris is a good choice.

When the black currant crop has been gathered the bushes should be pruned. Black currants fruit best on new wood, so shoots which have fruited should be cut right out. Some varieties produce strong new shoots on older wood. In this case the older shoots must be cut back to this point.

After pruning, feed with a general fertiliser at the rate of 4 oz. to each plant. This will help to ripen the young wood.

Cordon, espalier and dwarf pyramid apples should be summer pruned, both to keep them in shape and to check

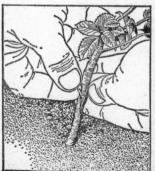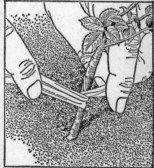

their vigour. The new sideshoots should be shortened to four or five leaves each, not counting the basal rosette of small leaves. Do not prune the main stems which are extending the length of the trees.

Cover Morello cherries with nets to protect the ripening fruits from birds.

VEGETABLES

Cabbage white butterflies are often present at this time of year, and caterpillars can be seen on cabbages and other members of the brassica family. Where possible, squash the eggs on the undersides of the leaves before any damage is done, and, in any case spray with derris.

Spray celery with a combined fungicide and insecticide as a protection against leaf spot and celery fly.

Runner beans will benefit from daily syringeing with water to assist the setting of their flowers. They should be watered freely in dry weather.

Outdoor tomatoes also need water in dry weather. Feed once a week with a good tomato fertiliser, as directed by the manufacturer, or a general fertiliser at the rate of 1 oz. per plant. Stop the plants at one leaf above the fourth truss.

Make further sowings of parsley and turnips.

GREENHOUSE

Seedlings of *Primula obconica* and *P. sinensis* should now be large enough for potting singly. Use the John Innes No. 1 Potting Compost. The plants can be put outside in a cold frame for the summer.

Rooted cuttings of Zonal pelargoniums required for winter flowering should be potted on now.

Spray tomato plants overhead each day to encourage the flowers to set. The ventilators should be closed while doing this and kept shut for half an hour. Afterwards, open the ventilators gradually to give the plants the buoyant atmosphere they require.

FLOWERS

Now is the time to begin to propagate many shrubs. Cuttings of half-ripe wood of such popular shrubs as forsythia, flowering currant, escallonia, weigela, deutzia and *Viburnum tinus* will all root easily. Pull off the shoots with a heel of older wood attached, trim this neatly with a sharp knife or razor blade, dip in hormone rooting powder and then insert the cuttings in sandy soil in a cold frame with a close-fitting light. Shade from bright sun.

Michaelmas daisies need secure staking for the flower sprays can become very heavy. The canes or sticks should be positioned in such a way that they do not interfere with the natural habit of the plants.

Sow seed of *Primula pulverulenta* and *P. japonica* as soon as this is ripe.

FRUIT

Continue to train wall-trained fruit trees, tying in the shoots which are to be retained as evenly as possible over the space available. This routine work is essential with peaches, nectarines and apricots.

This is the time to bud fruit tree stocks. Peaches, plums and other stone fruits are almost always increased by budding, and it is also a good method of increasing apples and pears; but it does mean that the necessary young rootstocks must be obtained during the autumn and winter.

It is now time to prepare the ground for new strawberry beds. As the plants will probably remain for two to three years (but no longer, see p. 85), the ground should be well dug and cleaned and thoroughly fed, both with well-rotted manure and bonemeal.

Any plum branches which show signs of silver leaf disease should be cut out at once and burnt. This disease, which causes a metallic silvering of the leaf, is not to be confused with mildew which produces a powdery white outgrowth on the leaves.

July: week 4

Melons in frames will need regular watering and feeding to swell the fruits.

When dessert cherries have finished fruiting, spray the trees against blackfly if this is still troublesome. Derris, malathion or menazon (a systemic insecticide) can be used for this purpose.

VEGETABLES

Brussels sprouts will benefit if a little soil is pulled up around the stems from each side of the row, much as one would earth up potatoes.

The planting of sprouting broccoli, kale and so on should be completed as soon as possible now and this is certainly the latest time to plant broccoli which are to head by spring. The plants should be spaced $2\frac{1}{2}$ ft. apart each way. Kale is extremely hardy, and the young shoots are eaten in late winter and early spring.

Cucumbers in frames will need a lot of water at this time of year and will also benefit from a weekly feed with a compound fertiliser. Remove the male flowers to prevent fertilisation of the female flowers. If this is not done the fruits will have a bitter taste.

Onions should also be fed for the last time. Sprinkle the fertiliser very thinly between the rows and then hoe it in carefully.

Shallots and garlic have now finished making their growth and should be lifted carefully and laid out in the sun to dry. Often, it is a good idea to cover them with cloches, or if an empty frame is available they can be put in this with a light over the top of them to protect the bulbs from rain – but keep the frame ventilated.

Any flower heads which appear on spring-sown parsley should be removed as soon as they are noticed.

Now is the time to gather herbs of all kinds for drying. Tie the shoots or leaves up in small bundles and suspend them head down in a cool, airy shed or room, not, for preference, in strong sunlight.

GREENHOUSE

Chrysanthemums which are now growing in pots standing out of doors will benefit from topdressing with a good, rich compost. A space was left for this topdressing and I would recommend using the John Innes No. 3 Potting Compost.

Camellias growing in pots should be fed once a week throughout the summer.

Tomatoes which are carrying heavy crops may also need feeding with extra nitrogen to help the top trusses. Dried blood can be used for this purpose, or sulphate of ammonia, but be careful not to give an overdose as this could easily cause severe leaf scorching. A teaspoonful of the fertiliser per gallon of water would be ample.

Sow seeds of Brompton stocks in seed boxes or pans and place in a cold frame.

At about this time of the year, old cyclamen corms can be started into growth again by watering them lightly. As new leaves appear, the plants should be repotted in fresh John Innes No. 2 Potting Compost, keeping the corms slightly above the surface of the compost.

Drying herbs for winter use by tying them together in bunches and hanging them upside down in a cool, airy place

August: week 1

FLOWERS

Dahlias should be disbudded, only one flower being retained on each stem. There is, however, no point in doing this with small-flowered varieties grown primarily for garden decoration, and it certainly should not be done with small pompons in which to have too large a flower is a fault. The plants will also need regular tying.

Unless outdoor-flowering chrysanthemums are being grown specifically for spray flowers I disbud them to one flower bud per stem. All the remaining buds should be rubbed away, and all sideshoots should be removed.

This is a good time to trim laurel hedges. For this, secateurs should be used and not hedge shears which would disfigure the foliage.

This is the latest time to plant colchicums (meadow saffrons), autumn-flowering crocuses and hardy, spring-flowering cyclamen. Colchicums produce their lovely lavender flowers before the leaves and the bulbs should be planted with a covering of 2 in. of soil. Where several bulbs are being planted, space them 12 in. apart and make sure that you choose a well-drained site. With cyclamen it is best to purchase pot-grown plants rather than dry tubers.

To enable light to reach the lower trusses of tomatoes and assist with ripening, some of the nearby leaves may be removed

Most lilies should be planted in November or in early spring, but the lovely Madonna Lily, *Lilium candidum*, is an exception and it must be planted during August. Do not bury the bulbs deeply – an inch of soil above them is ample.

Pinch back the unwanted growths on wisterias to keep the plants under control.

FRUIT
If black currants were not pruned and fed last month this job should be attended to straightaway. Take care when applying the fertiliser to keep it away from the young shoots as they are easily scorched.

VEGETABLES
Both runner beans and celery are crops which need a lot of moisture, and if the weather continues hot and dry they should be watered freely. Both will also benefit from feeding during early August. I like to use a solution of nitrate of soda mixed at the rate of $\frac{1}{2}$ oz. to a gallon of water, this to be given after normal watering.

By this time autumn-sown onions and those grown from sets should be making good bulbs and the tops are best turned over to hasten ripening. If the bulbs are partially lifted with a fork, this will also encourage them to ripen. This ripening process is important if the bulbs are to keep right through the winter.

Spray or dust the later peas with BHC as a preventive against thrips, and add a fungicide to control mildew. BHC should not be put on crops which are to be used within two weeks.

Spring cabbage seed may be sown in the Midlands and the North. Make a further sowing of lettuce for late autumn use.

Cucumbers growing in frames will need feeding as well as watering and I like to topdress over the roots with John Innes No. 3 Potting Compost. Cut the fruits regularly as they mature.

August: week 1

GREENHOUSE

Seedling calceolarias should be potted before they become overcrowded into 3-in. pots of John Innes No. 1 Potting Compost. They need cool, shady conditions.

At this time of year cyclamen in frames need to be sprayed overhead both in the morning and the evening. Close the frame immediately after the evening spraying but open it again just before dark. From August onwards, when the weather is warm, I take the lights off the frames completely in the evening to allow dew to get on the leaves.

Keep a careful watch on cinerarias for aphids and the leaf miner maggots which make white streaks in the leaves. If taken early the maggots can easily be killed with the point of a penknife or between the finger and thumb, but if the attack is severe, spray with malathion.

There is a delightful, fragrant, white-flowered jasmine, *Jasminum polyanthum*, which blooms in winter and is ideal for training up one end of the greenhouse. It needs this protection as it is not quite hardy. The flowers are pink at bud stage. Cuttings of this species can be rooted now in sandy compost in a propagating frame with a temperature of 18 to 21°C. (65 to 70°F.). Make the cuttings 4 in. long.

Some of the leaves must be removed from the lower part of tomatoes grown under glass to allow the sun to ripen the fruits, but do not remove too many at any one time or the swelling of the fruits will be checked.

Prick out cyclamen seedlings raised from a sowing made at the end of June when these are large enough to handle. Some seeds take several weeks longer than others to germinate, so do not discard the seed pan straightaway. Prick the seedlings out into boxes filled with John Innes No. 1 Potting Compost.

This is also the time to prick out seedlings of *Primula malacoides* before they become overcrowded. Put them into seed boxes of John Innes No. 1 Potting Compost and house them in a cold frame.

FLOWERS

To keep the garden neat and tidy and prolong the flowering season, cut off the dead flower heads.

Seed pods of hardy primulas and *Meconopsis betonicifolia* (*M. baileyi*), the lovely Himalayan Blue Poppy, are now ripening. The seeds will germinate better and more quickly if they are sown immediately. The seeds of hardy primulas can be sown out of doors in good, well-drained soil in a shady border. Meconopsis seed can also be sown out of doors in sheltered areas, but in my part of the country (Shropshire) I prefer to sow the seed in boxes placed in a cold frame.

As cordon-trained sweet peas reach the top of the canes the stems should be untied and lowered. Lay them along the ground and retrain them up canes five or six feet further along the row.

Winter-flowering pansies will now need pricking out. The young seedlings should be spaced 3 to 4 in. apart in a nursery bed. They should grow rapidly and make good specimens for planting in their flowering positions in October.

FRUIT

If strawberries are planted within the next few weeks the plants should carry a good crop next year. It is a common fault to plant too closely, and a distance of 2 ft. should be left between the plants and $2\frac{1}{2}$ ft. between the rows. It is most important to make sure that you obtain certified virus-free stock as strawberries are so prone to virus disease.

To assist the ripening of peach and nectarine fruits, move the leaves back to expose them to the sun. A label tucked behind each fruit will help to bring them forward. Keep the lateral growths pinched back.

Start to prune raspberries as they finish fruiting. The old canes which have fruited should be cut out to ground level and only six or seven of the strongest new canes retained. To prevent overcrowding, remove any young growths from the base of the stools.

With pruning completed, tie the selected new canes to the wires, and then apply a dressing of general fertiliser at the rate of 2 oz. per yard of row. Keep the fertiliser away from the canes, otherwise scorching is likely to occur.

VEGETABLES

Seed of spring cabbages can be sown now. This crop needs to be grown in good, well-worked but firm soil. Good varieties are Flower of Spring and Harbinger. The plants will be ready for setting out by the beginning of October. Space them 18 in. apart in rows 2 ft. apart.

A sowing of onion seed to provide plants for spring planting should be made now in a sheltered nursery bed. They need a deep, well-worked soil containing plenty of plant food. Suitable varieties are Ailsa Craig and Autumn Queen.

Make a sowing of the onion White Lisbon, too, this month if you want a supply of spring onions.

Potato blight must not be allowed to develop for if it does, not only will it spoil the potato crop, but it will also attack outdoor tomatoes. Spraying regularly with a copper fungicide will help to prevent serious damage to both these crops.

Start to blanch celery by earthing up the plants. Any small offsets should be removed first, and then newspaper is wrapped around the stalks and tied loosely with raffia to prevent soil getting to the heart. The earthing up should be done in easy stages, drawing up a little soil at a time over the next six or eight weeks until only the tuft of leaves at the top of the plants is exposed.

GREENHOUSE

Pelargonium cuttings should be potted without delay into 3- or 3½-in. pots using the John Innes No. 1 Potting Compost. Cuttings of *Genista fragrans* which have rooted need the same attention.

Pelargoniums needed for flowering in the winter are best stood out of doors for a few weeks so that the growths become well ripened. Small attentions like this make all the difference.

Seed of schizanthus can be sown. This is a lovely flower for a spring display and it is not difficult to grow in a cool house.

As old cyclamen corms begin to make new growth they will need watering more often as the plants will be filling their pots with roots. Cyclamen strongly dislike draughts so ventilate the greenhouse carefully.

Arum Lilies (*Zantedeschia aethiopica*) will now be making new growth. Leave them outside in a shady position until the end of the month when they will need dividing and repotting. Shake the old soil from the roots and then carefully divide them. Put three roots in each 8-in. pot and use the John Innes No. 2 Potting Compost. Water the pots well and then stand them in a sheltered position out of doors. They must, however, be brought into a cool greenhouse before there is any chance of autumn frosts occurring.

Some gardeners seem to think that ferns need no feeding. This assumption is quite incorrect and they should be fed regularly with weak liquid manure just like other plants during the spring and summer.

Earthing up celery plants. Note the newspaper collars which prevent soil getting into the heart

August: week 3

FLOWERS

Zonal pelargoniums are splendid summer bedding plants and also valuable pot plants. Cuttings of these plants can be rooted in two ways, either outside in a border, or in pots in a cool greenhouse.

Suitable cutting material can be taken from plants at this time of year without spoiling the appearance of the bedding display. Firm shoots must be chosen and when preparing the cuttings make a clean cut immediately below a leaf joint. Then root the cuttings either in a partially shaded border, with plenty of coarse sand added, or in 3½-in. pots of sandy compost in a cool greenhouse.

In both cases, when roots have formed the plants can be potted singly in 3½-in. pots of John Innes No. 1 Potting Compost, and kept in a cool greenhouse throughout the winter.

Earwigs can be a great nuisance on dahlia plants as they eat the flower buds. Hollow bamboo canes are often a favourite hiding place, so seal up the tops of the canes used to support the dahlias. Flower pots filled with hay and inverted on stakes amongst the plants make effective traps. Inspect them daily and dispose of the insects. Alternatively, spray or dust the plants with BHC.

Suckers which appear around roses should be cut off close to the rootstocks to prevent further growth. If necessary, draw back the soil to do the job properly.

It is now time to cut 'everlasting' flowers for drying. The flower stems should be tied into bunches and hung upside-down in a cool, dry, airy place, away from direct sunshine which would make the flowers fade.

Cutting of pinks which were taken last month will have rooted by now, and can be planted out in their growing positions. They like a good-quality, well-drained soil of a non-acid nature and an open sunny position.

FRUIT

Young growths on Morello cherries trained on walls should be kept in place and any unnecessary growths pruned out. The Morello cherry carries its fruit on young wood made in the previous year, like the peach and the nectarine.

Wall-trained plums must also be trained into position and either tied to the supporting wires or to nails in the wall.

Good, strong-growing strawberry plants in pots can be selected for forcing under glass next spring. The best plants can be potted now into 6½- or 7-in. pots using the John Innes No. 3 Potting Compost. Afterwards, plunge in a cold frame.

Some of the early apples ripen quite suddenly and are apt to fall off if they are not picked. Look over the trees daily and test the ripeness of the fruits by lifting them carefully. A fruit which is ready to be picked will virtually come away in the hand as soon as light pressure is exerted.

VEGETABLES
Marrows should be cut while they are young and tender and before the outer skin hardens and sets.

Seedlings of seakale beet and spinach beet should be thinned now to about 12 in. apart.

Vegetable marrows should be cut while they are still young, otherwise the skin hardens and sets. Note the pieces of slate under the marrows to protect them from the soil

August: week 3

Gather French and runner beans regularly while they are young and before they become old and stringy. A sowing of lettuce can be made out of doors now for planting later in a garden frame. Good varieties for this sowing are Cheshunt Early Giant, All the Year Round and May Queen.

In the North the ground can be prepared for spring cabbages. Fork over the soil lightly and apply a dressing of general organic fertiliser at the rate of 2 oz. per square yard.

As farmyard manure is scarce and expensive these days it is a good idea to sow a green manure crop now if there is any vacant ground in the vegetable garden or allotment. Rape or mustard are suitable plants and can be sown broadcast.

GREENHOUSE

Watch double-flowered begonias for signs of botrytis which may appear on the stems and where dead flowers have been removed. Treat with flowers of sulphur and by keeping the atmosphere of the greenhouse drier.

This is the time to pot plants of *Primula obconica* and *P. sinensis* into their final 5-in. pots, using the John Innes No. 2 Potting Compost. Afterwards, return the plants to the cold frame in which they are spending the summer.

The fibrous-rooted, winter-flowering begonias can now be given their final move into 6- or 7-in. pots if really large plants are wanted. Use John Innes No. 2 Potting Compost. Pick off any flowers which appear before the end of September to build up the strength of the plants. A minimum temperature of 16°C. (60°F.) is needed if the plants are to flourish.

Prick out Brompton stock seedlings into $3\frac{1}{2}$-in. pots and use the John Innes No. 1 Potting Compost. Return the plants to the cold frame for a week or two. They can then be bedded out in the garden except in very cold districts where it is safer to overwinter them in a cold frame.

FLOWERS

Border carnations and pinks layered during July should now be rooted and ready for planting in their flowering positions. Sever the young plants from their parents, and lift them with plenty of soil attached to the roots. In cold districts it is best to pot the rooted layers and keep them in a cold frame for the winter. Use 4-in. pots and the John Innes No. 1 Potting Compost.

As rambler roses finish flowering they should be pruned. Disentangle the growths from the trellis and cut out at ground level those growths which have carried flowers. Keep the new stems made this year and tie them neatly into place. These will bear flowers next year.

Cuttings of alpine plants put in earlier (see p. 81) and now rooted should either be planted out where they are to grow or be potted up and placed in a frame until spring. If they are to be kept in pots it is best to plunge them to their rims in sand, ashes or soil.

As soon as lavenders have finished flowering clip the bushes back to prevent them becoming bare at the base.

To be able to grow good plants the soil must contain liberal quantities of organic matter, and with farmyard manure so difficult to obtain nowadays it is most important that all waste green material from the garden should be saved for composting. From now on there should be quite a lot of garden waste and a compost heap can be built up in layers.

To ensure even decomposition of the heap, thoroughly water each layer and sprinkle with a proprietary accelerator or with sulphate of ammonia. After a few weeks turn the heap so that unrotted material on the outside is thrown into the centre. Keep the heap well watered.

FRUIT

Move back the foliage on cordon and espalier apples and pears to expose the fruit to the sun to ripen.

August: week 4

Any side growths which appear on the young shoots of peaches and nectarines should be nipped out.

As melons in frames begin to ripen a delicious scent is produced, and to assist ripening a warm, dry, atmosphere is needed. Damp, stuffy conditions may cause rotting, so ventilate more freely.

Runners formed on strawberries should be removed, also any dead or diseased leaves. Strawberries are very prone to virus diseases and as these are spread by aphids, it is wise to spray regularly to kill these insects. One of the best controls is malathion.

Water any newly planted strawberries to help them to become established in their new beds.

VEGETABLES

In the Midlands and South sow seed of winter lettuce.

Outdoor tomatoes will need frequent feeding now, and watering if the weather is dry. To help the lower trusses of fruit to ripen some of the foliage may be removed.

Brussels sprouts and other winter greens will benefit from feeding with a sprinkling of a compound fertiliser.

GREENHOUSE

Cinerarias in $3\frac{1}{2}$-in. pots should be ready for potting into their final 5- or 6-in. pots, using the John Innes No. 2 Potting Compost. Good drainage is important for these plants. With clay pots, this can be provided by crocks (pieces of broken flower pot) placed over the drainage hole, and if plastic pots are used, extra sand should be added to the compost. After potting, return the plants to the cold frame.

This is quite a good month in which to take cuttings of coleus, selaginella, pilea, tradescantia, zebrina, *Impatiens holstii* and its varieties. These need a close propagating frame but not necessarily a heated one.

Freesias and lachenalias are especial favourites with

many gardeners, and the corms and bulbs respectively should be potted within the next week or two.

To take the freesias, first, place seven or eight corms in a 6-in. pot of John Innes No. 1 Potting Compost and cover with about 1 in. of the mixture. Then stand the pots in a cold frame under a thick layer of moist peat. Remove the peat after about six weeks – by which time a good root system should have formed – and bring them into the greenhouse where they must be kept well ventilated. Such plants will flower in January.

With lachenalias, plant five to seven bulbs in a 5-in. pot of John Innes No. 1 Potting Compost and cover these also with about 1 in. of compost. Then move to a shaded cold frame and water very sparingly until the leaves begin to develop. They must then be brought into a cool greenhouse. More water will be needed as the plants come into flower. The flowering period is from February until May, and afterwards the plants are dried off and the bulbs ripened in the sun.

Chrysanthemum disbudding needs frequent attention. One bud per stem is the rule except for spray varieties.

Feeding outdoor tomatoes with a general fertiliser. Afterwards, it should be thoroughly watered in unless rain is expected

September: week 1

FLOWERS

The nights are getting longer and, one must assume, colder, so there will be a danger of fungi appearing on many of the bedding plants, particularly begonias. Dead flowers left on the beds will act as centres of infection so take care to remove them.

This is the time to take lavender cuttings and those taken with a heel root most readily. They can either be rooted in a sheltered bed out of doors or in sandy soil in a cold frame. Outdoors, make a shallow trench and sprinkle this with plenty of sharp sand before inserting the cuttings and filling in. These cuttings can be planted out in the garden the following spring.

Cuttings of roses can also be inserted now. Ramblers almost always grow well from cuttings and so do many of the old-fashioned roses and modern floribundas. One merit of roses on their own roots is that suckers become an advantage instead of being a nuisance.

Reduce the growth of herbaceous plants which have finished flowering but do not cut off too much foliage.

Continue to take cuttings of bedding geraniums (pelargoniums). Cuttings of bedding fuchsias can also be taken and rooted in pots of compost in a garden frame, but there is some urgency about doing this job as the weather will soon be against quick rooting.

Preparing cuttings of lavender from firm shoots of the current season's growth with a heel of older wood attached

FRUIT

Complete the planting of strawberries as soon as possible, otherwise the plants will not have time to establish themselves and build up strong crowns for fruiting next year. Strawberries can be planted in late summer, in early autumn or in March, but spring-planted ones should not be allowed to bear fruit during the first season.

If no proper fruit store is available then other arrangements must be made, for the apples and pears are now starting to mature. Tomato trays make ideal boxes for storing fruit in. It is also an advantage to wrap the long-keeping apples and pears individually, so buy some of the paper wrappers sold especially for this purpose.

Boxes of fruit must be stored carefully for they need to get plenty of air and they must be accessible so that the fruit can be inspected from time to time. Just one rotten apple can quickly spread infection.

Start to gather the early pears as they ripen.

VEGETABLES

Onions are late in ripening in some seasons, which is hardly surprising bearing in mind the unpredictable qualities of our climate. If the tops have not been turned over yet to expose the bulbs to the sunshine, do this now and lift the crops as soon as possible.

Gather French and runner beans regularly and never leave any pods on the plants to become old and stringy unless they are required for seed purposes, in which case they should be specially marked.

Continue to earth up celery, but remember that this should not all be done at once. It is far better to earth up the plants a little at a time.

Celery leaf spot can be a troublesome disease. It causes spotting on the foliage and this will shrivel and die in a bad attack. Spraying with a good proprietary copper fungicide will help prevent the disease spreading.

Sweet corn should be gathered before the cobs begin to

September: week 1

go too yellow. If the harvesting is left until later they may be rather mealy.

GREENHOUSE

The most forward cyclamen plants are now beginning to show some flowers, and these should be pulled off with a sharp tug. In this way, the flower stem should come away cleanly without leaving a piece at the base which could rot and cause trouble later on. At the same time remove any leaves which are showing signs of decay. Feed regularly each fortnight with liquid fertiliser.

Keep young schizanthus plants as near to the glass as possible so that the seedlings grow sturdily.

Insert cuttings of heliotrope and the verbenas Lawrence Johnston and Loveliness. These will root readily in sandy compost in a propagating frame with a temperature of 15°C. (60°F.).

There are many annual flowers which make excellent pot plants for the cool greenhouse, flowering from April to July or August. Antirrhinums, Beauty of Nice and East Lothian stocks, clarkias, cornflowers, godetias, nemesias and salpiglossis are all excellent for this purpose but they must have cool conditions. Seeds of these can be sown now in seed compost and germinated on a shelf near the glass in a cool greenhouse.

As soon as the seedlings can be handled, prick them out into 3-in. pots of John Innes No. 1 Potting Compost and place them on a shelf near the glass to pass the winter. When they are ready for another move, repot them into 5-in. pots. Some are better for stopping, the tips of the shoots being pinched out when they are about 4 to 5 in. high to encourage a bushy habit.

FLOWERS

If daffodils and narcissi are to be naturalised in grass, the sooner they are planted the better. A special bulb-planting tool saves much time and labour.

Clear away all hardy annuals which have finished flowering and put them on the compost heap.

Brompton stocks raised in a cold frame can be bedded out now in all but very cold districts. In such places it is better to overwinter them in a cold frame.

The growth of rampant climbers like some kinds of clematis, wisteria and ampelopsis can be cut back now if the plants are taking up too much room.

Tie in the long shoots which have been made during the past few weeks by climbing roses. They are the shoots which will flower most freely next year but they are rather brittle and easily broken by stormy weather.

Violas are best renewed frequently, either from seed or cuttings. Cuttings can be taken now and they should be prepared from young, non-flowering shoots. Insert them in sandy soil in a cold frame.

Outdoor hydrangeas should be treated now with one of the proprietary hydrangea colourants if blue flowers are required next year.

FRUIT

Continue to gather early apples and pears. Generally, these early-maturing varieties are not long keeping so they should be stored where access is easy.

Melons in frames should now be approaching ripeness and must be cut as soon as they become fully ripe. They can be kept for a short time in a cool larder and once ripe will certainly do better there than if they are left in the frame.

Prepare the ground for new plantings of raspberries and black currants. It is useless to retain diseased stocks of either of these fruits. Mosaic and reversion disease can soon ruin the cropping qualities of plants and if either trouble is apparent it is far better to clear out the whole

September: week 2

bed and replant with healthy stock. It is not wise to plant new stock on ground which has already been used for these fruits and a fresh site elsewhere in the garden should be chosen.

Now is the time to place grease bands around fruit trees. They are particularly effective on apples against the winter moth, the wingless females having to crawl up the trees in the autumn to lay their eggs. Broad bands of grease-proof paper are placed around the main trunk and are coated with a sticky substance, and insects which crawl over these are trapped.

Unwanted laterals should be removed from peaches and nectarines for the last time this season.

VEGETABLES

Onions which have been harvested should be placed in the sun to be sure of thorough ripening, but put them somewhere where they will be sheltered from rain. If part of a frame is available this is ideal.

Prepare the ground for spring cabbages if this has not already been done. Although this crop needs good soil it should not be too rich as this might encourage soft growth which could not withstand hard winter weather.

Store shallots in a cool, dry place. Select bulbs for planting next year and store these carefully, too.

Leeks can be fed with a general organic-based fertiliser at the rate of 2 oz. to the yard of row.

We have now reached what must be considered the latest date for gathering herbs for winter drying, so if this work has not already been completed it should be attended to immediately.

Marrows can be stored if there are too many for immediate use. A good way of keeping them is to hang them in nets in a place which is cool and frost proof.

GREENHOUSE

As cinerarias, *Primula obconica* and *P. sinensis* fill their 5-in. pots with roots they should be fed regularly until the flower buds have formed.

Seedling cyclamen should be potted singly in small pots by now. Use the John Innes No. 2 Potting Compost with extra sand added to ensure good drainage.

If cyclamen plants are in frames, leave the lights off at night so that the plants get the benefit of the heavy autumn dew.

Arum Lilies should be housed by now to avoid any possibility of frost damage. Water the plants sparingly until growth really gets under way. The temperature can be raised gradually to 13 to 16°C. (55 to 60°F.) as the plants develop if early flowers are desired. If you are prepared to wait longer for the blooms a temperature of 7 to 10°C. (45 to 50°F.) is all that is needed.

Blackcurrant leaves, showing the effect of reversion. On the left an infected leaf with only three veins to the lobe. On the right a healthy leaf with five veins

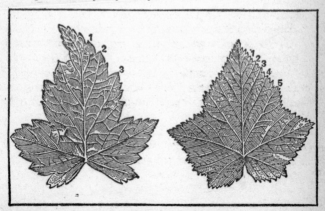

September: week 3

FLOWERS

As the flower spikes of Red Hot Pokers (kniphofias) fade, cut them off for these soon look unsightly.

This is about the time to take cuttings of both bedding calceolarias and penstemons. The cuttings should be prepared from non-flowering shoots and will root readily in sandy soil in a cold frame. They should be over-wintered in the frame and planted out in April.

Winter-flowering pansies may already be producing flowers but I prefer to pick off these early blooms to help the plants make stronger growth before winter.

Hardy primulas are all the better for being planted rather early in the autumn. *Primula japonica* and *P. pulverulenta* and their varieties look particularly attractive when planted near to water.

Choice alpines are best protected during the autumn and winter by a sheet of glass. These plants are not averse to cold but cannot stand wetness.

FRUIT

Different varieties of apples and pears reach maturity at different dates so it is important to watch each tree carefully. Do not gather late-keeping apples like Sturmer Pippin, Blenheim Orange and Bramley's Seedling too early or they will shrivel in store.

Young peach and nectarine trees sometimes become too vigorous and make a great deal of growth at the expense of fruit buds. This can be checked by lifting and replanting the trees now.

The ordering of fruit trees should not be left any later than this if they are required for planting in the autumn. However, if you intend to buy container-grown plants this is another matter.

Grapes on outdoor vines should be exposed to the sun by folding back the leaves or, in some cases, by actually removing a few of them.

Loganberries should be pruned by cutting out the canes which have just borne fruit and training in their place all the young canes which will fruit next year. The canes should be cut out at ground level so that no short stumps are left.

VEGETABLES

Carrots should be lifted and stored before the roots split, which they will do once the autumn rains begin.

For the same reason beetroot are better lifted and stored now – in boxes between layers of moderately dry sand or soil, the containers being housed in the garden shed. The ideal size for a beetroot is that of a cricket ball. Carrots can be stored in the same way.

Lettuces sown last month for frame cultivation should now be ready for planting, and more seed can be sown.

GREENHOUSE

Where possible, clear away tomatoes so that the house can be prepared for the autumn and winter flowers. Any unripened fruits can be put in boxes to ripen indoors.

Cyclamen which have been growing in a frame would be better in a greenhouse now as there will soon be a danger of frost at night. Keep the plants well ventilated and do not use any artificial heat yet.

Tuberous-rooted begonias and gloxinias should be

Protecting alpines from winter rain and dampness with the aid of a pane of glass supported on wooden pegs

September: week 3

gradually dried off as they finish flowering. The pots can be placed on their sides under the staging.

All manner of spring-flowering bulbs, including daffodils, may now be potted or placed in bowls for late winter or spring flowering. You can have colour from Christmas until spring in the cool greenhouse from daffodils (narcissi) and hyacinths.

For the earliest flowers of narcissi you need to grow varieties like Paper White or Grand Soleil d'Or, and remember that the attractive Roman hyacinths flower earlier than the large-flowered kinds. Pre-cooled bulbs will also be in flower by Christmas.

If these bulbs are grown in pots place them close together and use John Innes No. 1 Potting Compost. With potting completed, the tips of the bulbs should be just above the surface of the compost.

If they are to be grown in bowls use bulb fibre, making sure that it is well soaked before use. Whichever method is used, do not pot too firmly or the roots may push the bulbs out of the compost.

For the next 8 to 10 weeks the pots or bowls should be stood in a cool, sheltered place outside. Give them a thorough watering before covering with a layer of sand, weathered ashes or peat. By the end of November the bulbs should have made good root systems and be ready for moving, first to a cold frame and, then, when the flower buds appear, into a greenhouse or warm room.

Young hydrangeas which are housed in cold frames should be covered with lights at night from now onwards. They must be returned to the greenhouse in October.

Prick out schizanthus seedlings singly into small pots of John Innes No. 1 Potting Compost and place on a shelf near the glass for they like plenty of light.

FLOWERS

The propagation of all the more tender bedding plants such as pelargoniums, fuchsias and iresines must be completed before the first frosts arrive. Cuttings can be prepared from firm, non-flowering shoots and will root easily in a warm propagating frame.

Cuttings taken earlier will need potting into 3½-in. pots of John Innes No. 1 Potting Compost. They should be brought into the greenhouse for overwintering.

Tuberous-rooted begonias used as bedding plants must be lifted before they are damaged by frost. Dry the tubers off and dust with flowers of sulphur before storing them in boxes of peat in a frost-proof place.

Seedlings of meconopsis raised from a sowing made in August should now be ready for pricking out into boxes. These should be overwintered in a cold frame and be planted out next April or May.

The earliest gladioli will die down soon and they should then be lifted carefully, ready for drying and storing in a frost-proof shed. When the foliage has died down it should be cut away. Save the cormlets or spawn which develop around the corm for growing on.

There are several ways of growing sweet peas and one is to treat them like autumn-sown hardy annuals, sowing the seed now out of doors where the plants are to bloom next year. A sheltered and well-drained border must be chosen, and the seed should be sown in a trench 2 to 3 in. deep for protection. Alternatively, sow 5 or 6 seeds in a 3-in. pot and germinate in a cold frame. The young plants will be potted in January.

FRUIT

Continue to pick apples and pears as they become ready. Storing pears can bring problems. I like to store mine where I can look over them at intervals of a few days, for pears have a habit of ripening and then going soft in two or three days. This is why there are so many complaints

September: week 4

of pears being 'sleepy' before they are ripe. In fact they were ripe first but this period was missed.

When the soil is sufficiently dry, hoe between strawberries to encourage growth and build up strong crowns.

The amount of pruning carried out on damsons should be minimal, but when it is necessary this is a good time to do it, before the leaves fall.

VEGETABLES

Continue to earth up celery, a little at a time. If the earthing up is done too quickly it will tend to check growth unduly. Soil should also be pulled up along each side of the leek rows. Alternatively, if extra long blanched stems are required, a couple of boards can be fixed on edge to each side of the row and the space in between filled with soil.

Onions can be stored in ropes or on slatted shelves in a dry, airy shed or room. Make sure that they are well cleaned (but not skinned) before storing.

When the skin of maincrop potatoes has set, that is when it cannot be easily rubbed off, the tubers are ready for lifting.

Gather all outdoor tomatoes, even if they have not ripened yet. There is always a danger of frost from now onwards and the fruits would be ruined by even a degree or two, so it is far better to finish the ripening indoors. I find that a warm, dark place such as an airing cupboard, will quickly ripen green fruits.

GREENHOUSE

Seedling freesias, which up to now have been standing in a frame, will be better in a greenhouse. They should be given plenty of light and ventilation. The same thing applies to winter-flowering pelargoniums.

Perpetual-flowering carnations will also be better in the greenhouse. They like plenty of light and air and a rather dry atmosphere, but not too much heat. If large flowers are preferred, the plants should be disbudded.

As soon as the greenhouse has been cleared of tomatoes, any chrysanthemums showing prominent flower buds may be brought inside. Before doing this, remove all dead leaves and spray the plants with a combined fungicide and insecticide. When they are in their new quarters, allow them plenty of space and ventilate freely.

On cold, damp nights provide the greenhouse with a little artificial heat.

Pot up crocuses, chionodoxas, scillas and other early bulbs for the spring and plunge out of doors. Crocuses should not be forced before mid-January, when a temperature of 10°C. (50°F.) is sufficient.

Bring plants of *Azalea indica* back into a cool greenhouse. Also cinerarias and plants of *Primula malacoides*, *P. obconica* and *P. sinensis*.

Annuals raised from a sowing made in the greenhouse at the beginning of the month will need pricking out.

Before pot-grown chrysanthemums are brought back into the greenhouse they must be thoroughly sprayed with a combined insecticide and fungicide

October: week 1

FLOWERS

Damaging frosts may occur at any time now. Indeed, it is probable that even before October arrives frosts will have occurred in cold districts. Bearing this in mind, make the fullest possible use of all the flowers while they last.

Lawns will benefit from a good raking and aerating, as well as a topdressing of equal parts of peat and loam brushed well into the surface.

If frost threatens, the more tender plants like pelargoniums and fuchsias must be brought inside. Some of the fibrous-rooted begonias (*Begonia semperflorens*) can also be lifted and put into pots, as they will go on flowering in the greenhouse throughout most of the winter. They will also provide stock for future use.

Rambler roses should be pruned and trained if this has not already been done. Cut out as much of the growth which has already flowered as possible.

FRUIT

The gathering of apples and pears must continue as the various varieties become ready for picking.

Handle all fruit with care and only store really sound fruits.

In a wet summer raspberries often throw up more basal growths than usual and it is wise to cut some of them away. Canes which will carry next year's crop must now be tied permanently in position.

Take gooseberry cuttings from firm young growths produced this year. Make a clean cut above a bud at the top, and below a bud at the base, finishing up with a cutting of about 9 in. in length. All the buds should then be removed, except the top three or four, to ensure that the bushes are grown on a short stem or 'leg'. After preparing the cuttings, insert them outside in trenches where the soil is light and well drained. A layer of coarse sand on the bottom of the trench will encourage rooting.

VEGETABLES

Lettuce seedlings can be planted in the frame to give winter supplies. After planting put down a slug killer to make certain that slugs and snails do no damage to the young plants. The frames should be ventilated freely whenever the weather is mild.

Gather all sizeable, ripe marrows before there is any danger of frost and store in a dry, frost-proof shed.

Maincrop potatoes should now be lifted and stored. It really pays to take advantage of every fine day and get this job done. As you pick up the tubers any that are diseased should be kept away from those being stored.

Make the most of the last of the runner and French beans by picking all the sizeable beans each day, particularly if frost threatens.

Late sowings of French beans made in June should be covered with cloches.

Take advantage of the dry weather which often occurs in early October to earth up celery for the last time. It is much easier to do this job when the soil is fairly dry rather than muddy and sticky.

Spring cabbages should be planted now. It is important to firm each one well in after planting. I like to draw out

Raking the lawn with a wire-toothed rake will remove dead grass and other debris, and also help to aerate the soil

October: week 1

drills with a hoe and plant in these. Then a little later I draw the soil back into the drills, so pulling it around the stems of the cabbages.

GREENHOUSE
Continue to bring chrysanthemums into the greenhouse as the flower buds form. If frost threatens they should be brought inside at once whether the buds are showing or not.

The Winter Cherry, *Solanum capsicastrum,* is another tender pot plant which will need protection as soon as there is a danger of frost. In fact, it is wiser to bring the plants in a week or so too early than to risk having them damaged.

Ventilate the greenhouse freely to keep air on the move and prevent too damp an atmosphere occurring which might encourage disease.

From now onwards, cinerarias will need very careful watering. They must not be allowed to become dry, nor must they be kept constantly sodden.

Arum Lilies which are growing strongly will need adequate water supplies and should be fed generously. They respond to regular feeding once the pots are full of roots. To obtain really good flowers, feed with a liquid or soluble feed once every 7 to 10 days.

Make a regular practice of picking off dead or decaying leaves from pelargoniums for if this is neglected disease can spread to the stems themselves.

It is not normally possible to buy pre-cooled bulbs before this time, but as soon as they arrive, pot them up and stand them in a cool place, preferably under a north-facing wall, until the third or fourth week in November. Cover them over with peat or weathered ashes in the normal way.

FLOWERS

This is the time to start planting out wallflowers, poly-anthus, forget-me-nots, Sweet Williams and foxgloves for spring bedding. Do not retain summer bedding flowers so long that these plants have insufficient time to establish themselves before the winter sets in.

Before the spring- and early-summer-flowering plants are put in, the soil should be dug over to the depth of a spade and a dressing of bonemeal applied at the rate of about a handful per square yard. The soil must be made firm and should be raked level before planting. Firmness is really important as it helps the plants to establish themselves.

Half-ripe shrub cuttings taken during July and August should now be rooted. I prefer to pot these into 3½-in. pots and keep them in a frame for the time being. When they are well established they can be plunged outside.

FRUIT

Apples and pears in store need careful watching as they may show signs of brown rot or other diseases, even if they appeared perfectly sound when gathered.

It should now be possible to complete the picking of apples and pears. It is dangerous to leave them on the trees too long as storms could bring them down.

Do not delay in the preparation of sites for fruit trees which one intends to plant in November. The soil should be well dug and, enriched with some decayed manure plus a good sprinkling of coarse bonemeal.

This is the time to prune blackberries, the method being exactly the same as that used for loganberries. Old canes which have just borne a crop are cut out and young canes are trained in to take their place.

Remember that autumn gales are often severe and badly tied growths of blackberries and loganberries may be broken, with the inevitable loss of much fruit next year.

October: week 2

VEGETABLES

Keep a close watch on potatoes and onions in store and remove any which show the least sign of disease.

Choose any day when the soil is reasonably dry on top to hoe between spring cabbages and winter lettuces.

The lifting and storing of late-sown carrots and beetroot should now be completed. Both vegetables can be stored in a cool shed in boxes of sand or ashes.

This is a good time to dig in green manure crops like mustard. It is quite a good policy to sprinkle the crop with Nitro-chalk as it is turned in, as this helps it to decay quickly and improves the quality of the resultant manure.

In very exposed places it may be necessary to put stakes to the Brussels sprouts, especially after a wet summer and if the soil is light. Remove any yellowing leaves from the plants to prevent attack by fungus diseases.

GREENHOUSE

The latest flowering chrysanthemums should now be brought inside before they are damaged by frost. The same applies to fuchsias.

Make a regular practice of looking over cyclamen and removing any leaves which are showing signs of decay, otherwise diseases can spread easily to the young buds in the crowns. Continue to feed cyclamen plants with weak liquid manure at fortnightly intervals.

When the foliage of gloxinias and begonias has withered completely, knock the tubers out of their pots and shake away the old compost. Then dust the tubers with flowers of sulphur and store them in a dry, frost-proof place.

Calceolarias must not be allowed to become pot bound. Pot them on as soon as the small pots become comfortably filled with roots, and keep them as near to the glass as possible to prevent the growths from becoming drawn. The plants will be repotted into 5-in. pots at this stage, using the John Innes No. 1 Potting Compost.

Specimens of *Genista fragrans* will also need moving into 5-in. pots from the 3½-in. pots in which they were potted in August. The John Innes No. 2 Potting Compost should be used.

Hydrangeas in pots which have been in a cold frame during the summer should now be moved to the greenhouse. Well-grown plants can be potted on into 7-in. pots.

Do not provide too much heat in the greenhouse at this time, just sufficient to keep the air dry and on the move. This will prevent the atmosphere becoming damp and stagnant.

Freesias raised from corms started into growth in August should now be moved from the cold frame into the cool greenhouse. They need support and twiggy sticks are ideal for this purpose. These plants will come into flower in January.

As with carrots, beetroots are readily stored in boxes of dry sand in a frost-proof place. Beetroot tops are best removed by twisting them off rather than cutting, as this lessens the chance of bleeding

October: week 3

FLOWERS

When planting bedding material for spring, take great care to preserve as many roots as possible. This job is often done in far too much of a hurry, with the result that a lot of the roots are lost, and the plants suffer a severe setback.

Aubrietas and *Alyssum saxatile*, such excellent plants for rock gardens, dry walls and the tops of retaining walls, can now be planted safely. Winter-flowering pansies can be used for the same purpose.

Dahlias can be left in the ground until their tops have become blackened by frost, but if the ground is wanted for other purposes there is no reason why they should not be lifted at once. The tops should be cut off 9-in. above the tubers, which must then be dried off thoroughly before they are stored.

Cuttings of many shrubs and roses may be taken now and rooted outside or in a frame. It will be a year before they are sufficiently well rooted to be lifted and planted elsewhere, so the cutting bed should be in a place where the cuttings can be left undisturbed.

There are hardy heathers of varying kinds in flower throughout the year, and this is the best time to plant

When gathering the leaves of seakale beet it is best to take only a few from each plant, which otherwise will be weakened

them. For winter flowering, *Erica darleyensis* can be relied upon to show its deep rosy-pink flowers from November onwards. Then, for winter colour also, there are all the varieties of *E. carnea*. These, like *E. darleyensis*, will grow in an alkaline soil provided plenty of peat is added. Plant them $1\frac{1}{2}$ ft. apart and put plenty of the same variety together to get the best effect. Good varieties include the pure white Springwood White and the bright pink Springwood Pink, both 6 to 9 in. tall; and the rich carmine Eileen Porter of similar height. This last flowers the winter through, and the other two from January to April.

FRUIT

Strawberry beds should be cleaned up, all dead, diseased and damaged foliage being removed. Then, if the soil is dry enough, hoe between the young plants. With strawberries, as with spring cabbages, it is an advantage to draw up a little soil along each side of the row. Alternatively, topdress with well-rotted manure.

Tie in raspberries but do not, as yet, cut back the tips, a job better left until mid-February. Make quite sure that the supports for the raspberry training wire are in good condition and not rotting at the base.

Prune and tie in Morello cherries. The object is to retain as many of the good young branches made in the past summer as possible and to reduce all older side growths which have already borne a crop. Morello cherries, like peaches, bear best on year-old laterals.

VEGETABLES

I know just how difficult it is for most amateur gardeners to get supplies of animal manure these days, but I would stress again its value in the garden. As an alternative or supplement to manure, compost is excellent. Compost heaps made earlier in the autumn should now be turned, bringing the material on the outside into the centre and vice versa.

October: week 3

When pulling the leaves of seakale beet take a few at a time from each plant. If the plants are stripped completely they will be weakened.

GREENHOUSE

Dry off the last of the begonias and gloxinias growing in pots by turning them on their sides. Achimenes in pots can also be dried off as these, too, must have a thorough rest during the winter.

Gradually reduce the amount of water given to fuchsias, but do not allow them to become completely dry. Rooted cuttings from which specimen plants and standards are to be formed should be potted on as necessary.

Another plant that may need potting up is *Primula malacoides*, the dainty winter- and spring-flowering primula. They should be moved into 3½-in. pots and the John Innes No. 1 Potting Compost should be used.

Pot up lilies such as *Lilium auratum* and *L. speciosum rubrum* for greenhouse use. Both are stem rooting and the bulbs should be kept well down in the pots. These need not be filled completely yet as some topdressing will be desirable later. The pots should be put into a cold frame for the winter, and then returned to a cool greenhouse with a temperature not higher than 10°C. (50°F.) in March or April.

This is the time to propagate lilies from scales. Insert them upright in a mixture of peat and sand, covering to a depth of ½ in. and place in a cold frame. By the following autumn bulblets will have formed at the base of the scales. These are removed and potted up.

Generally speaking the atmosphere in all greenhouses will have to be kept drier from now onwards.

FLOWERS

In many places autumn colour is now at its best, and this is a good season to bring out the garden notebook and jot down the names of shrubs which have especially attractive berries and autumn leaf colour. Some of these, perhaps, can be planted in one's own garden.

Now is the time to begin cleaning up the herbaceous border. Many gardeners argue that it is better to leave the dead tops on the plants for winter protection but I am not in favour of this. I prefer to have all top growth trimmed back and the borders properly cleaned and pricked over before winter. At the same time take up all the canes used for support and store them away in a dry place.

When frost has browned the tops of dahlias cut them down to within 9 in. of ground level. Tie a label to each stem so that the plants can be easily identified at planting time next year. Lift the tubers carefully and spread them out, stalk end downwards, in a frost-proof shed for a week or two to dry before they are finally stored away for the winter.

Most bulb planting should be completed as quickly as possible, although tulips can be left until November. Nevertheless, even with tulips, I think that better results are obtained from planting in October.

Planting tulips between forget-me-nots for spring display

October: week 4

The best tulips for the average garden are the Early Single and Early Double varieties. The tulip species are also excellent, and these can be left in the ground from year to year. For example, *Tulipa kaufmanniana*, the Water-lily Tulip, has many fine March- to April-flowering hybrids. These have an excellent colour range, they are only 6 to 8 in. tall and are splendid flowers for the rock garden or the front of the border.

FRUIT

Inspect all fruit in store and remove any which show signs of decay. By inspecting fruit regularly it is possible to make use of much which would otherwise become rotten and spread decay to healthy fruits.

It is a good plan to select some of the really sound, late-keeping apples such as Bramley's Seedling, Newton Wonder, Crawley Beauty and Laxton's Superb, wrap them separately and store them away for winter use.

Many small gardens have little room for top fruits, but there are few in which at least some soft fruits cannot be planted. In a week or so it will be time to plant gooseberries, currants and cane fruits so prepare the ground for them by digging and manuring.

VEGETABLES

Carefully lift a few roots of parsley with plenty of soil attached and transfer to a frame for winter use.

Brussels sprouts which show a tendency to be late and are not producing their buttons well can be encouraged by feeding now with a general fertiliser. Any leaves which have turned yellow should be removed. Winter cabbages, too, will benefit from a dressing of general fertiliser.

The top growth of Jerusalem artichokes can be cut down to ground level. Celeriac, by contrast, should be lifted and stored in damp sand in a shed for winter use.

Round-seeded peas can be sown under cloches in flat-bottomed drills 8 in. wide and 2 in. deep. Sow the seeds 2 to 3 in. apart in three rows.

GREENHOUSE

At this time of year one appreciates more than ever having shelves in the greenhouse near to the glass. Such a shelf is the ideal place in the autumn for young schizanthus plants, calceolarias and annuals being grown for spring flowering.

Cinerarias need plenty of air so give them as much ventilation as you can. The tops of some of the plants can be pinched out to delay flowering and so give a longer overall display.

Pinch out the tips of the tallest schizanthus seedlings to encourage the formation of bushy plants.

Pot plants must be fed less and less frequently now, with the exception of cyclamen and primulas.

Roses can be lifted and potted for flowering in the greenhouse during the spring. Any roses already in pots should be pruned back fairly hard and topdressed with fresh, rich compost.

After flowering, herbaceous plants should be cut down with secateurs and the soil between the plants lightly pricked over

November: week 1

FLOWERS

Before the weather becomes too bad to do any serious gardening, get as much tidying up done as possible.

This is the ideal time to lay turf. It must be said, however, that making a lawn from turf is much more expensive than making a lawn from seed, and good turf is difficult to get hold of.

Lily bulbs can be planted when conditions are suitable, the only exception being *Lilium candidum* which should be planted in August. *Lilium regale*, the Regal Lily, is a species I am particularly fond of, and others include *L. auratum*, the Golden-rayed Lily of Japan and *L. tigrinum*. I also like the many splendid hybrids, including the Mid-Century Hybrids, the Golden Clarion Strain and the Bellingham Hybrids.

Lilies like a well-worked soil with good drainage. They also need a cool root run, so the lower parts of the stems should be shaded from strong sunshine by interplanting with herbaceous plants or low-growing shrubs.

Stem-rooting lilies must be planted rather deeper than non-stem-rooting kinds – at a depth of 8 to 9 in. as opposed to 5 to 6 in. And to avoid trouble with bulb rotting, it is always a good idea to put a little sand in the bottom of the planting hole on which the bulb can rest. I plant

Planting lily bulbs on a bed of sand. For the most effective display they should be planted in groups of three or four

the bulbs in groups of three or four of the same kind as the flowers look more impressive this way

Shrubs which are a little tender, like crinodendrons, the evergreen ceanothus and the hebes should be protected now. Bracken is ideal for this purpose as it is light and does not retain rain water like straw.

The blue-flowered agapanthus likes a well-drained position which is also open and sunny. It is another of those plants which needs winter protection, so before really severe weather arrives I always put bracken, straw or peat around and over the crowns.

Now that the mowing season has finished the lawn mower, of whatever type, should be cleaned, greased all over and put away in a dry place. If it appears to need an overhaul or if the blades need sharpening, now is the time to get this done.

FRUIT

Ground should now be prepared for the planting of all kinds of fruit trees, bushes and fruiting canes. Dig the soil over as deeply as possible and work in some manure. This is particularly important in the case of black currants.

Fruit trees trained to walls, fences and so on should be pruned now. After pruning see that all branches and shoots are securely tied.

Inspect the posts carrying wires for raspberries and blackberries to make sure they are still sound. Where posts have decayed at ground level they can be made good by driving into the soil a length of angle iron and bolting this to the base of the post just above ground level.

When contemplating the purchase of new fruit trees do not forget that a quince may be a useful addition, not only for the value of the fruits for jellies and flavouring but also for the attractive foliage of the tree.

Now is the time to prune red and white currants. Cut back the leading shoots to leave about 6 in. of the new season's wood, and cut back the sideshoots to leave one bud.

Cuttings of red, white and black currants can be taken now. These hard-wood cuttings, made from the current season's wood, should be about 10 in. long and be planted 9 in. apart in a trench of sufficient depth to cover all but the top three or four buds when filled in. Often, the lower buds of red and white currants are removed so that the plants will grow on a leg.

VEGETABLES

It will be possible to work heavy clay soils more easily next spring if they can be ridged or turned over and left as rough as possible so that a large surface of soil is exposed to the weather.

Keep an eye on lettuces under cloches and in frames, and do not let quick-growing weeds like chickweed smother them. Lettuces need plenty of air circulating around them to keep them healthy.

Lift and store Jerusalem artichokes in the same way as potatoes so that they are accessible if the ground freezes.

Also lift a few parsnips and store these in damp peat or sand in a shed for use later on.

If it is too wet to work outside, this is a good time to give all the cloches a thorough wash and clean. This job is too often neglected. Light transmission is a vital factor in plant growth.

GREENHOUSE

Crowns of lily-of-the-valley can be potted in John Innes No. 1 Potting Compost to flower early in the spring in a cool greenhouse. Just cover the crowns with soil.

Cyclamen and winter-flowering primulas are already coming into flower and will benefit from feeding once a fortnight with weak liquid manure.

Pot schizanthus as soon as they have filled their pots with roots and place them near the glass.

FLOWERS

The roots of outdoor chrysanthemums should be carefully labelled and then lifted and brought into the greenhouse or frame for the winter. I put mine in boxes, cover the roots with a little soil and then place them in a frame.

If no greenhouse or frame is available, the chrysanthemums may be kept quite safely if the boxes are placed under the shelter of a wall and covered over with a little straw, bracken or even sacking during periods of severe weather.

Lily-of-the-valley crowns can now be planted out of doors. They do well in a partially shaded position such as under a north-facing wall or even beneath the shade of trees. Plant the crowns singly, 9 in. apart with the points just below the surface. They need good, fairly light soil.

Cut the dead flower spikes from Red Hot Pokers (kniphofias), then draw up the foliage over the centre of each plant and tie it together like a tent. This will help to keep moisture away from the crowns and so prevent losses due to rotting. In very exposed gardens put straw over the crowns as an added protection.

This is a good time to plant hedges. Quickthorn makes a good boundary hedge, but the hedging plant *par excellence* is *Cupressocyparis leylandii*. This conifer grows extremely quickly, has the most handsome deep green foliage and will make a splendid formal hedge measuring anything from 8 to 25 ft. in height in a relatively few years.

Other attractive conifers for hedging purposes are the Lawson's Cypress (*Chamaecyparis lawsoniana*) and certain of its varieties like Green Hedger; and the Western Arbor-vitae, *Thuja plicata*. I do not like privet because it robs the soil of nourishment and needs clipping at least three or four times during the growing season.

For hedges inside the garden *Rosa rugosa* will make a really big hedge and provide a display of flowers for many weeks in summer. Also very vigorous is the hybrid tea rose Peace.

For smaller hedges many floribundas are excellent, as well as some shrub roses. Floribundas include Queen Elizabeth and Iceberg; and shrub roses for this purpose include the hybrid musk Penelope, and the modern shrub rose Elmshorn. An old garden rose to consider is the rose-pink Frau Dagmar Hastrup. The freely produced flowers are followed by large crimson hips.

For seaside hedges there is no better shrub than *Euonymus japonicus*, a tough evergreen with deep green, glossy leaves which can withstand a salt-laden atmosphere. This will make a formal hedge 10 to 12 ft high.

FRUIT

This is the time to start pruning apples and pears. Cordon-trained trees will need a good deal more pruning than bush trees. In many cases bush trees are badly over-pruned with the result that they make too much new leafy growth the following year and do not fruit well. It is far better to thin out the branches than to cut back every shoot.

The sooner the planting of fruit trees and bushes can be done the better. This will allow them to become established before the severe weather sets in. But planting can continue until March, if necessary.

If your garden is small, be sure to obtain apples and pears on dwarfing or semi-dwarfing rootstocks. Single-stemmed cordons or small bush trees are more suitable than large bushes or standards and produce high-quality fruit.

VEGETABLES

Get as much of the winter digging done as possible before the soil becomes too wet and sticky, leaving the ground as rough as possible, especially if the soil is heavy. The greater the surface area exposed to frost, wind, and rain the better. Never under any circumstances, though, try to work the soil when it is in an unsuitable condition for this can do much damage to its structure.

In many parts of the country where the winters are not too severe, broad beans can now be sown out of doors. This crop need a rich, well-manured soil and the drills should be made 3 in. deep and 2 ft. apart, the seeds being set 4 to 6 in. apart in the drills.

This is also a suitable time to sow a hardy, round-seeded pea such as Meteor, or Feltham First, but again a sheltered position and a well-drained soil are essential.

GREENHOUSE

The October-flowering chrysanthemums have now finished their display and the growths should be cut down to within 9 in. of the pots. These stools will later provide young shoots from which cuttings can be made.

Remember that calceolarias should be quite dry before they are watered again. Indeed, this remark applies to all pot plants at this time of the year except those which are in full and rapid growth in heated greenhouses.

When digging, the soil should be left in large lumps to expose it to the action of frost and rain

November: week 3

FLOWERS

All this month while the weather remains open and the soil is in good condition the planting of trees and shrubs may continue. It is important to stake trees firmly and I like to drive a stake into the planting hole before the tree is put in position. This not only results in firm staking but it also ensures that the stake will not be driven through the roots. While it is advisable to have manure or compost in the soil this should not come in contact with the roots. Put it down below them so that the new roots can go in search of it.

Good flowering trees for gardens include most of the ornamental crabs such as the purple *Malus lemoinei*; the rosy-crimson *M. eleyi* with purplish-green leaves; and *M. floribunda* with crimson buds and pink flowers. These flower in April and May. Attractive dark-coloured fruits are carried later in the season by *M. lemoinei* and *M. eleyi*. The Japanese cherries are among the best of all flowering trees for the garden for to their display of flowers in spring must be added their delightful leaf tints in autumn. Three popular varieties are the rose-pink Hisakura; the erect-growing Amanogawa; and the double-flowered Shirofugen, pink when in bud and white later. Then there is the attractive Autumn-flowering Cherry, *Prunus subhirtella autumnalis*, which will bear its delicate little semidouble, white flowers on and off from this month until March. These are just a handful of the huge number of varieties to choose from.

Waterside plants such as astilbe and trollius can be planted, but this is not the time to move true aquatics.

The compost heap will need turning regularly.

FRUIT

This is a suitable time to deal with old and neglected fruit trees. With these, there should be no snipping of innumerable small shoots, but rather the complete removal of a branch here and there to open up the centre of the tree and let in light and air. All large wounds made in this way should be trimmed carefully with a sharp knife and then painted to prevent disease from getting into the tree. Look carefully for canker wounds on these old trees and cut out the affected parts. Then paint the wounds over with a bituminous paint.

Fork very lightly around fruit trees and bushes to get rid of weeds, but do not dig deeply as this would destroy many of the feeding roots near the surface.

By now most of the leaves should have fallen from fruit trees and these can be raked up and placed on the compost heap. This will be another stage in the pre-winter clearance I have already mentioned.

This is a good time to plant red and white currant bushes in ground prepared during October.

Continue the winter pruning of apples and pears.

VEGETABLES

In frosty weather it is a good plan to wheel all manure or compost onto the ground now, in preparation for digging in later on. Do not spread it out but leave it in large heaps until the digging is carried out.

Hoe between winter lettuces whenever soil conditions permit, and also between rows of autumn-sown onions.

Pot-grown bulbs being moved from the plunge bed and brought into the light

November: week 3

Remove any yellowing leaves from Brussels sprouts and leaves which have fallen to the ground. When picking sprouts, gather only a few at a time from each plant. Start from the bottom and work upwards.

Early savoy cabbages are now coming into season and my advice would be to use these first and leave the sprouts as long as possible.

GREENHOUSE

By now the weather will, no doubt, be wet, cold, and, in many places, foggy as well. This is often very trying for plants under glass and I want to emphasise the importance of avoiding an excess of atmospheric humidity. Stop damping the floors of the greenhouse, do not overwater the plants and do all you can to keep the air dry.

The earliest varieties of evergreen azaleas – not to be confused with *Azalea indica*, the Florists' Azalea – which may be expected to bloom by Christmas or soon after, should now be brought inside.

Strawberries in pots at present plunged out of doors should have their yellowing and dying leaves removed as well as any late runners which may have formed. The plants do not need a great deal of water now, but they should not become really dry.

Bulbs in pots which have been plunged outside for 8 to 10 weeks may now be brought out into the light. They should not be given too much warmth straight away, and a cold frame would be an ideal position. Give them a further week or so to become accustomed to the change and then take them into the warmth of the greenhouse to bring them into flower. I like to see the flower buds above the bulb before I begin to force them in the greenhouse.

FLOWERS

This is a good time to inspect garden paths and repair or re-lay any which are in need of attention. Old gravel paths will be greatly improved by the addition of a little fresh gravel. If you are planning new paths it is wise to remove the soil to a depth of several inches along the length of the path, using it to build up beds, borders and so on, and to replace this with stone, broken bricks or other hard rubble, which will make a good solid foundation for the path.

Fork lightly between shrubs to get rid of weeds, aerate the soil and work in any leaves which may be lying on the surface. There is no need to remove annual weeds in a mistaken enthusiasm for cleanliness, as forked in they will rot and make excellent humus. Do not fork more than 2 in. deep.

Rhododendrons and azaleas may be planted now, but do not plant these shrubs where there is any free lime in the soil. If you are in doubt on this point, have a sample of soil tested or test it yourself by using one of the soil testing kits which you can buy at garden centres. This will give you precise indications of the soil's acidity or alkalinity.

Put frame lights or cloches over some of the Christmas roses (*Helleborous niger*) to bring the flowers on for Christmas and keep them free of mud splashes.

FRUIT

This is a good time to plant raspberries, blackberries and loganberries. For those who object to thorns, thornless varieties of the latter two are available. Malling Promise, Malling Jewel and Malling Enterprise are all good varieties of raspberry. Merton Thornless is a very good blackberry. It is not too vigorous and the fruit is of excellent quality. Another good one is Himalaya Giant. Blackberries are very useful for continuing the soft fruit crop through into the autumn. LY59 is the strain of loganberry usually grown.

November: week 4

At any time between this month and March all three of these fruits may be propagated; the raspberries by division of mature plants and the blackberries and loganberries by layering.

Watch young fruit trees, particularly those planted in grass, for any signs of barking by voles, field mice or in country districts, rabbits. If such damage is allowed to take place it can easily prove fatal to the trees. Sacking dipped in animal oil and lightly placed on the ground around the trees, but not actually touching them, should keep these pests away.

Make an inspection of fruit in store, particularly late pears, and remove any which show signs of even the slightest damage. Pears which are beginning to mellow should be taken indoors for use.

Get on with the winter pruning of fruit trees and bushes as weather permits. Many fruit growers prefer not to prune plums, damsons and cherries in winter as there is then a greater danger of infection by silver leaf disease.

Using a soil-testing kit

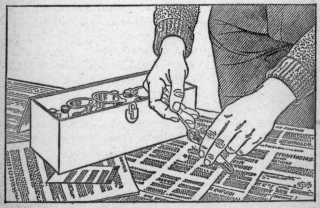

VEGETABLES

It may appear that I repeat myself rather about looking over stored potatoes, but it is so important to do this that it bears repetition. Look them over now and remove any diseased specimens, remembering that in a week's time – if this job is left – there may be twice as many spoilt.

Take every favourable opportunity to get on with winter digging, particularly on heavier soils. If you are bothered by couch grass, remove the roots while digging.

Lift a few crowns of rhubarb for forcing and leave them on top of the ground for a week or so before taking them inside and putting them under the greenhouse staging. The crowns can be packed close to one another and a little moist soil should be worked in among the roots. Forcing is more successful if light is excluded and to do this sacking can be hung from the top of the staging to the floor.

GREENHOUSE

Rooted pelargonium cuttings may be potted immediately or, if preferred, left in their pots until February.

With the exception of the Christmas- and Easter-flowering Cacti all cacti should be kept almost dry now. They need little or no water until the end of February.

The Christmas Cactus, *Schlumbergera buckleyi* (also known as *Zygocactus truncatus*), and the Easter Cactus, *Rhipsalidopsis gaertneri*, must be kept slightly moist during the winter months. They flower from November to January and from February to April respectively.

Young plants should be kept on a shelf as near to the glass as possible. On my shelves at this time of year are schizanthus, antirrhinums, various annuals, seedling cyclamen, *Primula malacoides*, and rooted cuttings of heliotrope. None of these needs much heat, but they should be protected from frost. Schizanthus need staking now.

Move prepared bulbs from the plunge bed into a cold frame. They should stay there for one or two weeks.

December: week 1

FLOWERS

Frosts in November usually finish off the last of the rose blooms, and to avoid them looking untidy during the winter I always cut the flowering growths on mine half-way back. This does not mean that the roses have already been fully pruned but that the soft top growth with a few buds and frosted flowers have been removed. The rose beds look all the better for this tidying-up and the bushes are less likely to be rocked by winter winds.

It is really very unwise to attempt to plant trees and shrubs when the soil is wet and sticky. In fact, it is best to keep off the soil altogether at such times.

If there is plenty of humus-forming material in the soil this will help to rectify deficiencies of soil texture – whether the soil is too heavy or too light. In the first case it keeps the soil more open and improves drainage and in the second it acts as a sponge-like medium to retain more moisture. Farmyard manure, peat, leafmould, spent hops and garden compost will all have this beneficial effect and may be worked in at any time during the winter.

This is a difficult time of year for plants in frames as these structures will probably have to be covered at night to keep out the frost, and on frosty days it is not wise to uncover them at all. They should, therefore, be ventilated whenever possible.

Herbaceous plants sometimes suffer badly during the winter from slug damage, and delphiniums are particularly likely to be victims. A good preventive is to scrape some of the soil away from around the crowns of the plants and replace this with sharp cinder ashes.

This is a good time to repair rustic fences, arches and similar structures, for you will be far too busy to attend to these matters in the spring.

At this time of year, too, I always think that it is a good idea to look at the garden with a cool eye and decide whether there is anything you want to change – or some new feature which you wish to introduce. Everybody these days is looking for ways to reduce maintenance work and any replanning on these lines could well be done now.

Shrubs of any kind are labour saving but the ground-covering kinds are particularly so. Heaths (ericas and daboecias) and heathers (callunas); *Cotoneaster adpressus praecox* and *C. horizontalis*; varieties of *Potentilla fruticosa*; the prostrate *Euonymus fortunei*; *Ruscus aculeatus* (Butcher's Broom); the late-winter-flowering *Sarcococca humilis*; and *Vinca major* and *V. minor* (the periwinkles) are just a few of those useful for this purpose.

Then there are herbaceous plants like the hostas, so showy with their bold, often variegated foliage; the bergenias, again with bold foliage and handsome flowers; *Stachys macrantha superba*, with dark green, wrinkled leaves and rosy-purple flowers in June; tiarellas, tellimas, pulmonarias, herbaceous geraniums, astilbes and a host of others.

If new plant features incorporating this kind of plant are to be created, then the planting should all be completed between now and next spring.

FRUIT

It is now easy to distinguish the buds on black currants which are affected by the big bud mite, for these buds will be large and globular in contrast to the smaller and more pointed healthy ones. All affected buds should be picked off and burnt. It is important to do this job thoroughly. Prune outdoor vines by cutting back all last year's branches to two eyes and removing all thin and useless wood. Severe annual pruning will keep the plants under control.

VEGETABLES

Celery should be lifted as it is required for use.

When the ground is dry, pull a little soil up around the stems of spring cabbages. I find that this helps to bring the plants through the winter safely.

December: week 1

GREENHOUSE

As chrysanthemums finish flowering, they should be cut back and the stools put as near to the glass as possible. Alternatively, they can be put into a cold frame.

Take all the stools out of their pots, shake the soil away from them and then pack them close together in boxes, covering the roots with fresh potting compost. Take care to label the stools to prevent any confusion over varieties.

Cyclamen should now be almost at their best, and they must be watered with care. Watch for signs of botrytis in the crowns. Pull out any decaying leaves and dust the crowns with flowers of sulphur to stop the spread of fungus.

Examine all bulbs plunged in ashes or in dark places. By now, some of them may be ready for moving into a cold frame.

Bulbs which have been out of the plunge bed for some time can be brought into a warm house or heated frame. It is best to bring them in in stages, a few at a time, so that a succession is maintained as far into the spring as possible. I like to see the flower buds showing well above the bulbs before I even start to force them, otherwise the flowers may not develop properly.

Pre-cooled bulbs should be moved into the warm greenhouse to bring the flowers on for Christmas.

Dusting a cyclamen with flowers of sulphur to control an attack by botrytis. Any affected leaves or buds should be removed

December: week 2

FLOWERS

Many winter-flowering shrubs start to bloom now and in my part of Shropshire both *Viburnum fragrans* and *V. tinus*, the Laurustinus, often make a lovely picture at this time. Although many flowers may be damaged by November frosts other buds soon open. *Erica carnea*, the winter-flowering heather, and some of its varieties like the rosy-pink King George, are usually in flower, and *Prunus subhirtella autumnalis* – which I consider the best of all winter-flowering trees – can always be expected to bloom just now.

Wooden trellis work and fences should be examined and, if necessary, treated with a good wood preservative. Do not under any circumstances use creosote as this is liable to damage plants growing nearby.

Twigs of numerous trees and shrubs, including those of the yellow-flowered *Jasminum nudiflorum*, will be in flower by Christmas if cut and put in water in a warm room. When cutting trees and shrubs in this way, take care not to disfigure them. The yellow jasmine, incidentally, is an ideal plant for training on a wall or fence and it will thrive in shade as well as in sunny places.

As long as the weather remains open and the soil conditions are good the planting of trees and shrubs can continue. Make sure that all trees are properly staked and that climbers are tied securely to their supports.

Especial care should be taken when staking trees for if the trunk is allowed to rub against the stake then the whole exercise is wasted. The proprietary plastic tree ties one can buy are especially good, for they hold the trees securely, well away from the stake, they are easy to put on and they are not expensive.

Establishing evergreen trees and shrubs is always a little tricky for they have no proper resting period and are in a particularly vulnerable position until their roots are active again. It helps tremendously if a screen of some kind is erected on the windward side after planting and left in position for at least the first winter. This could be made out of wattle hurdles or hessian, and the idea is to break up the force of the wind, which is one of the most damaging causes of moisture loss through the leaves. Also, a strong wind always tends to rock plants – even if they are well staked – and a tree or shrub struggling to re-establish itself will not like this at all.

FRUIT

Tar oil or DNOC winter wash should be ordered now because winter spraying is a job which must be started soon. It can only be done efficiently in fairly still, dry weather, and often there are not many suitable days during late December and January.

Burn all tree prunings as some may be infected with disease or be carrying the eggs of aphids or other pests.

Inspect all grease bands on fruit trees to make sure that they are still doing this job efficiently. Remove any leaves found sticking to the grease bands and renew the grease if necessary.

VEGETABLES

See that frame lights are properly tied down or firmly fixed in some other way for at this time of year they can easily be blown off and broken by strong winds. Cloches are usually able to take care of themselves, but some of the lighter types may require something to hold them down. It may be necessary to protect frames and cloches with sacking or straw at night if the weather is frosty.

The Brussels sprout harvest should be in full swing now. Do not remove the tops of the plant till the sprouts have all been gathered and only pick a few of the best.

Some of the winter broccoli are beginning to form their curds now. Turn in the leaves to protect the curds from frost and cut regularly, as once they have reached their full size they soon begin to spoil.

If seakale beet plants are covered with cloches they will provide leaves for winter use.

GREENHOUSE

If you want really large exhibition onions next year now is the time to sow a variety like Selected Ailsa Craig, Flagon or Premier. Sow the seed very thinly in a seed box filled with seed compost and germinate in a greenhouse with a temperature of 13°C. (55°F.).

Sponge the foliage of large-leaved evergreen plants such as dracaenas, codiaeums, ficuses and palms. If half a teaspoonful of milk is stirred into a cup of water it will put a nice gloss on the leaves. Alternatively, use a proprietary leaf-shining preparation.

Do not start to take chrysanthemum cuttings too early. There is sometimes a temptation to do this when good-looking shoots begin to appear in December. I prefer to leave all chrysanthemum propagation until early January and I am certain that the plants are better for it.

Light is especially important in the greenhouse at this time of year, and the glass should be washed – particularly on the outside – to remove any grime.

Protecting a newly planted evergreen with a hessian screen

December: week 3

This week embraces Christmas and I hope that all readers will have a happy time.

While comfortably seated beside the fireside there is an opportunity to consider what the garden has been able to contribute to the Christmas festivities. Are there a few chrysanthemum blooms, one or two pot plants or even some flowering shrub material which can be used? What vegetables has the garden provided for the Christmas table? Are there Brussels sprouts, cabbages, beetroot, onions and parsnips? Are there a few late dessert apples or some cooking apples? If not, now is the time to think ahead and make preparations so that you will have your own flowers, fruits and vegetables for Christmas next year.

FLOWERS

If snow comes early to give a white Christmas, do remember the damage that this can do to trees and shrubs. After a heavy fall get out into the garden and dislodge any large accumulations, especially on conifers which can be permanently disfigured if too weighed down.

If alpines have been covered with panes of glass, examine these and make sure that dead leaves have not collected under the glass and smothered the plants. Clear away any such leaves or rubbish and make certain the glass is secure.

When cutting evergreens for Christmas decoration use a sharp pair of secateurs and cut in such a way as not to disfigure the tree or shrub.

Garden frames should be painted regularly to keep them in good condition.

If frost has loosened the soil around cuttings these should be firmed in.

FRUIT

As soon as Christmas is over make preparations for winter spraying. Tar oil washes are particularly valuable for clearing the trees of lichen and moss. DNOC winter wash is even more effective than tar oil against some of the overwintering pests, but it does not clean the bark of the trees to the same extent. For these reasons it is quite a good policy to alternate the use of these winter sprays.

Apply sulphate of potash to fruit trees at the rate of 4 oz. per tree. This is a fertiliser which encourages fruit-fulness and good ripening.

VEGETABLES

It is a good plan to lift a few leeks and heel these in somewhere handy so that they can be reached easily if the weather turns really severe. Treated in this way they will keep in good condition for many weeks. It might be wise to lift some celery, too, and put in a frost-proof place.

More roots of rhubarb can be brought into the green-house for forcing. The best place for them, as I have already said, is under the staging where light can be ex-cluded with sacking, polythene, boards or other suitable material.

Many gardeners use the same part of the garden each year for growing runner beans and there is no harm in this provided the soil is well prepared. Make the trenches 2 to 3 ft. wide and 1½ to 2 ft. deep, and ridge the soil up

Forcing rhubarb under the greenhouse staging. Sacking or black polythene is hung from the staging to exclude light

December: week 3

on each side of the trench now. This will leave it open to the beneficial effects of the winter weather.

GREENHOUSE

Vines under glass should now be pruned. All side growths or laterals are cut back to two buds. The spurs carrying these shortened growths should be well spaced – at least 15 to 18 in. apart – on the main rod so that there is no overcrowding in the summer. After pruning, lower the rods to encourage even growth later on.

At this time, also, rub off the loose bark on vines as this forms an ideal hiding place for overwintering eggs of aphids and red spider mites. Scrape this loose bark carefully with a knife or twist it off with the hands. Care must be taken not to expose the green rind underneath.

Peach trees under glass must also be pruned, the method used being to cut out some of the older branches and train in younger wood in its place. Any diseased branches should be cut out.

Fuchsias are now dormant and they should be inspected periodically. Do not allow them to become too dry – just keep the soil slightly moist. Those plants being trained as standards should be tied to canes already placed in position so that the leading shoot grows straight upwards.

In heated greenhouses sprinkle water under the staging occasionally to prevent the atmosphere becoming too dry.

Start to take cuttings of perpetual-flowering carnations and continue to take these in batches until March. What is wanted is firm growths taken from non-flowering side-shoots, and those from midway up the flowering stems are best. These cuttings root best in pure sand in a propagating frame with a temperature of 16°C. (60°F.). As soon as the cuttings have rooted they must be potted into John Innes No. 1 Potting Compost, for sand on its own contains no nutrients.

December: week 4

FLOWERS

So we reach the last week of the year when we must begin all over again and plan and work for the year ahead. My advice to everybody is to try and arrange things so that work is reduced to a minimum, without loss of efficiency. Then the garden becomes a quiet retreat from the bustle of everyday life.

If the roots of hardy primulas have been exposed by heavy rain or lifted by frost, topdress the plants with a compost consisting of loam, peat and sand.

It is a good idea to get orders for flower seeds in early, so start thinking about them now. Many perennials can be raised from seed as well as half-hardy and hardy annuals, and biennials.

Half-hardy annuals I would not be without include zinnias, stocks, asters, French and African marigolds, ageratum and petunias. The hardy annual order is bound to include sweet peas, calendulas, candytuft, godetias, clarkias, the annual chrysanthemum and coreopsis, nasturtiums, scarlet flax and sweet alyssum.

Perennials which can be very successfully grown from seed are Oriental poppies, geums, gaillardias, *Campanula persicifolia*, lupins, delphiniums, anthemis, *Lychnis chalcedonica*, pyrethrum and aquilegias. Nor must we forget, of course, hollyhocks and Sweet Williams, which many gardeners prefer to treat as biennials, and foxgloves and Canterbury Bells which are genuine biennials.

Dig over borders and beds in which hardy annuals are to be sown in the spring. I do not recommend the use of any manure on such sites as long as the soil is reasonably good. Annuals flower best in a soil which is not too rich. Overfed, they produce mostly foliage.

Inspect all the sacking, bracken, straw and other material being used to protect tender plants and make sure that these protective materials are still in position and capable of doing their job.

December: week 4

FRUIT

Stop planting fruit trees and bushes if the weather becomes too severe.

Watch carefully for bird damage on fruit trees and bushes. Gooseberries and plums are particularly liable to suffer in this way, and sometimes birds will peck out all the buds. With small plants a fruit cage is really the ideal answer, but sometimes it is possible to make the buds distasteful to birds by spraying them with a bird repellent, applied as directed by the manufacturer.

Wall-trained fruit trees are always liable to suffer from lack of moisture during the summer and it is a good idea to fork manure, compost or peat in around the trees now to make the soil more moisture retentive. Do this job carefully, though, for it is easy to damage the roots.

If the weather is favourable – which means not frosty or windy – complete winter spraying with tar oil wash.

VEGETABLES

Lift a few roots of mint, place them in a fairly deep seed box, cover them with potting compost (old potting compost will do) and then put them in a frame or greenhouse to provide shoots for early picking.

If the onion bed has not already been dug and manured, no time should be lost in completing this task. It will then be broken up by the hard frosts which are still to come. Spread bonfire ash liberally over the top if this is available, as well as bonemeal and hoof and horn, each of which should be applied at the rate of 4 oz. to the square yard. The fertilisers will be worked in later when the seed bed is prepared.

GREENHOUSE

Cut back old pelargonium plants, shortening the growths to a joint or bud 6 to 9 in. above the pot. Then repot the plants, shaking all the old soil from the roots and putting them in the smallest pots which can take the roots comfortably. Use John Innes No. 1 Potting Compost.

I begin preparations for seed sowing in the greenhouse now by thoroughly cleaning all the pots, boxes and crocks and making certain that suitable supplies of seed composts are available. It is at this time of year that the value of a warm propagating frame for raising seedlings is most appreciated. What is needed is something in which a temperature of 16 to 18°C. (60 to 65°F.) can be maintained.

Now that the chrysanthemums have finished flowering there is more room to move around and the greenhouse can be thoroughly washed down, section by section, with a solution of disinfectant. Make sure that you get the scrubbing brush well into all the cracks and crevices and thoroughly clean the glass, both inside and out.

Continue to pick the dead leaves off plants in frames and in the greenhouse as these can encourage fungi.

I hope that you have enjoyed a profitable year's gardening and that you have found these notes useful.

Bracken, held in place by split canes, gives tender plants good protection

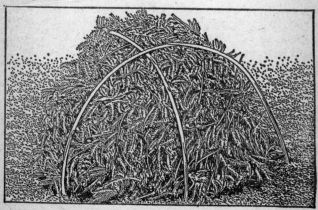

Index

d = line drawing

159